An olo.éditions production
www.oloeditions.com

Concept & selection
Nicolas Marçais
Philippe Marchand

Editing
Nicolas Marçais

Graphic design
Philippe Marchand

Authors
Béatrix Foisil-Penther
Claire Chamot

Layout and visuals
Fanny Naranjo

Published by Vivays Publishing Ltd
www.vivays-publishing.com

This edition © 2011 Vivays Publishing Ltd

ISBN 978-1-908126-03-0

English translation: Rae Walter in
association with First Edition Translations
Ltd, Cambridge, UK

Edited by Andrew Whittaker

Printed in China by Imago

CRAZY
DESIGN

Vivays Publishing

The breadth of objects in this book reflects the remarkable scope of contemporary design. Tables that look like mutant spiders; shopping trolleys reinvented as chairs; a chandelier made from old pens – the progressive, amusing, audacious and downright dotty collection of products illustrates the tremendous creativity and boldness at work. Many of the objects stand at the crossroads where sleek, classic design encounters the radical and the surreal. In common, behind the good looks, behind the humour, each item has a clearly defined function. We've chosen five powerful current trends to group and explore the designs: reproducing the natural world; inspired by recycling and salvage; inventing a new reality; escaping from a dream world; and transforming objects. So, turn on the anatomical lamp, settle down in your Bibliochaise with an ergonomic mug resting on your knee, and prepare to be surprised.

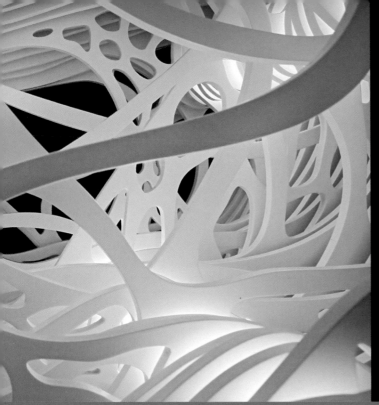

1

Reproduce

Create things
that are similar or
identical to a model.

2

Recycle

Salvage what
would otherwise be
wasted or unused
in order to make it
into something new.

3

Invent

Create or discover something new for a particular purpose.

4

Dream

Give free rein to your imagination, become absorbed in your wishes and desires.

5

Transform

Modify the meaning or function of an object, give it an entirely new function.

REPRODUCE

The natural world and its inhabitants (plants, animals and humans) provide designers with an inexhaustible source of inspiration. From spiders to trees, human limbs to clouds, the organic, naturalistic and cellular shapes permeate contemporary design. Equally, as consciousness of the Earth's fragility grows with every new revelation about climate change, so the design world becomes more aware of materials and manufacturing processes and their environmental impact.

ON YOUR FARM

Spurred on by the enthusiasm of Sofia Lagerkvist, Charlotte von der Lancken, Anna Lindgren and Katja Sävström of the Swedish collective Front Design, animals are entering the home. They're arriving in the shape of dark, elegant, utilitarian sculptures: the Horse Lamp, the Rabbit Lamp and Pig Tray. It's like a design-conscious version of *Animal Farm*, but minus the noise and the totalitarian dogma. The Horse Lamp base, moulded in black polyester and measuring 2.1m high by 2.3m long, attracted a lot of attention at the Milan exhibition in 2006, and, as you can probably imagine, having a near life-size equine lamp in the room is a guaranteed conversation starter.

ANIMALS HAVE LONG INSPIRED THE QUARTET AT FRONT DESIGN. INDEED, THEIR FIRST MEDIA SUCCESS CAME WITH A SERIES CALLED DESIGNED BY ANIMALS. WHETHER IT'S WALLPAPER, COAT-PEGS OR LAMPS, THE ANIMALS THEMSELVES PLAY AN INTEGRAL ROLE IN THE PRODUCT'S EVOLUTION. ONE PROJECT USED RATS TO NIBBLE OUT A PATTERN IN WALLPAPER.

LOOKSIE GRASS

REPRODUCE | **JOEL ESCALONA & STEPHEN CROWHURST** | www.joelescalona.com

PLAYING FIELD

This intriguing mat has been developed by Mexican designer Joel Escalona, in collaboration with Canadian artist and illustrator Stephen Crowhurst, to channel the kids' energy onto a somersault-friendly surface. The only sensible (or should we say 'grown-up') thing about the Looksie Grass (and it does look rather like mutant grass) is its size, fitting easily, as it does, into the average living room. The 'grass blades', measuring about 20cm high, allow your children to roll around in perfect safety. The little monsters can bounce, jump, fight or just sprawl around until they're exhausted. The mat is portable, so you can set it up wherever suits best – in the garden, bedroom, school playground or day nursery.

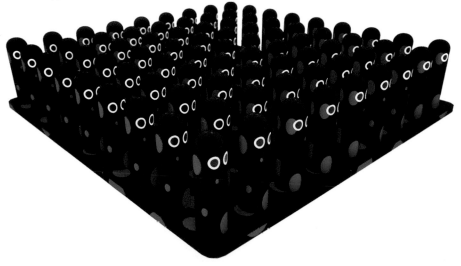

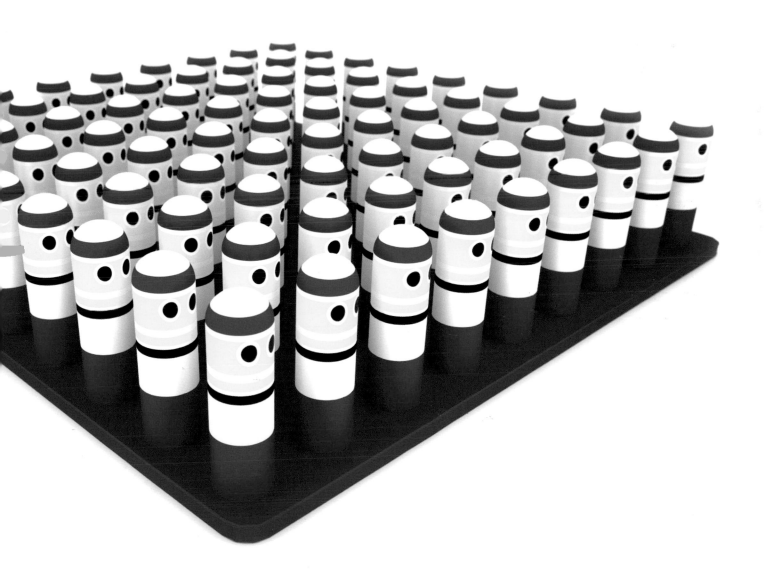

THROUGH-THE-WALL COAT-HOOKS

The outside world is coming in; the forest creeping through the walls and into the house. Or at least that's how it feels with Max Lipsey's branch shaped Coat Hooks. They create an otherworldly atmosphere in which the wilds are fighting back, reclaiming the urban environment. The aluminium branches come in small, medium and large sizes, with each individual piece numbered and signed by Max. Leave a stark, solitary branch emerging from the wall or gather a cluster together to create the illusion of a tree growing through the plaster. Each coat hook is highly polished at the tip, creating the effect of a mirror and bringing an added sparkle to whichever wall you deem worthy of the steely foliage.

THE 501 CHAIR

The iconic jeans become an iconic chair. London-based Israeli designer Assa Ashuach redefines the form and function of everyday objects, twisting perceptions to create a new kind of beauty. For Assa the holy grail is to reduce design to its bare essentials. It's a quest for simplification pushed along by the use of cutting-edge technology. The 501 Chair is the culmination of a long-term project that re-imagines the cult American jeans. The chair blurs the boundaries between a traditional seat and the standing position, enabling users to rest and relieve the tension in their backs. The shape of the chair encourages a new, more comfortable seating position, better adapted to the natural form of the human body, in contrast to traditional chairs that create the 90° angle between seat and back.

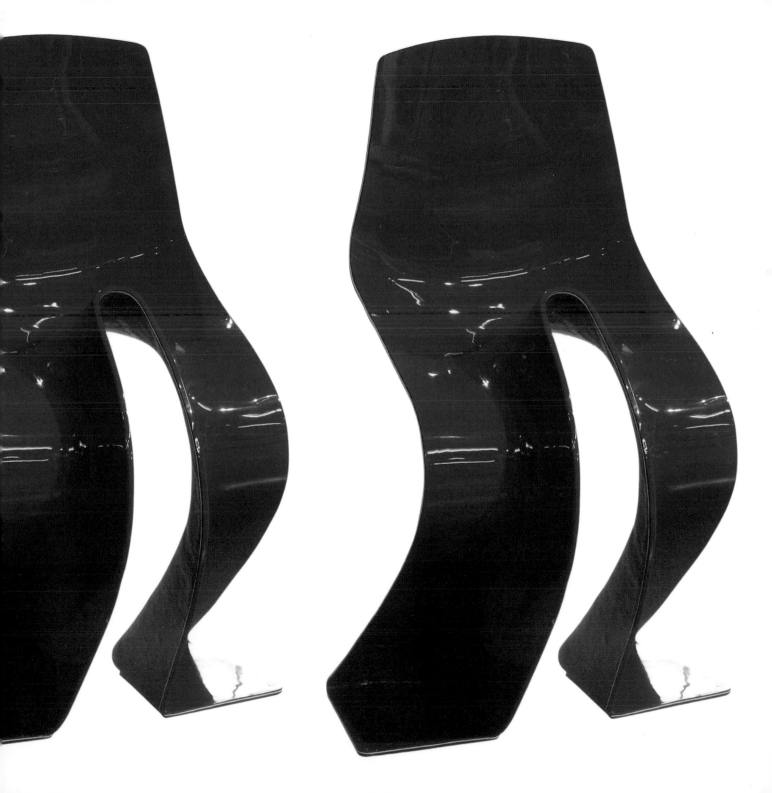

COAT HANGER

GET HOOKED ON BRANCHES

Can't see the wood for the trees? Perhaps this series of coat stands will bring some clarity of vision. At the very least they'll add a sense of fun to the house. They come in various guises – for adults or children, with or without leaves. The leafless tree is called (appropriately enough) Winter, whilst other versions go under the names of Grove, Grove Baby and Autumn. Created by Thai designers Panatda Manurasda and Chaiyapruk Tongcham of Studio Bo, the Coat Hanger trees fall under the banner of organico-poetic design. The guiding principle at Studio Bo has always been to imbue design with humour and positive thought, an ambition wholly realised here. We just hope you've got enough coats to do them justice.

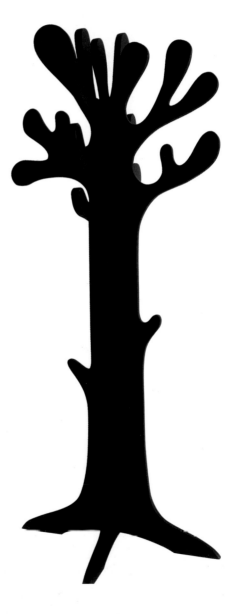

SPIDER TABLE

Arachnophobes beware! The Maxwell brothers, a pair of English designers working together under the auspices of Wayne Maxwell Design, took inspiration for the Ulwembu Coffee Table from the enormous rain spiders they saw in Africa. The eight-legged giants would invade their living room every time the heavens opened. They're not dangerous, but the spiders made enough of an impression to inform this elegantly designed table of bent, darkly wooden legs and clean glass top. The results may be sleek and modernistic, but they still stir a certain uneasy feeling; the suspicion that the table might get up and crawl across the room at the first sniff of rain.

ANOTHER SPIDER TABLE FROM AN ENGLISH DESIGNER, THIS ONE CLEVERLY COMBINES METAL, SILICON AND GLASS. CHRIS MURPHY PAID PARTICULAR ATTENTION TO THE ERGONOMICS OF THE DESIGN, CREATING A TABLE THAT, WITH JOINTED LEGS, IS EASY TO FOLD AND UNFOLD. IT COMBINES OPTIMUM PRACTICALITY WITH FUTURISTIC GOOD LOOKS.

REVIVALS

Prickly pair

The Cactus is a design classic; a cult object no less. Designed by the Italian duo of Guido Drocco and Franco Mello in 1972, the prickly, decorative coat stand has a steel body coated in a lacquered polyurethane foam skin. It was first re-issued in 1986, in a limited production run of 2,000, and has duly become a coveted collector's item. This, the 2007 re-issue, stands 1.7m high and 70cm wide, resplendent in beautiful grass green just like the original. For the first time, the Cactus is also available in its birthday suit, blanched of its green verve in a limited white run of just 250.

Cactus
Drocco & Mello
www.gufram.com/multiple/cactus.html

Designers have always been influenced by nature. When Drocco and Mello created their Cactus coat stand in 1972, they simply reproduced what they saw in front of them, adding their own personal touch and making it functional. The naturalistic movement, which was very much the 'in' thing in the 1970s, has endured in the form of a whole range of objects that have been re-worked many times since then and rejuvenated with the help of new materials or shapes. Today, such pieces have taken on a new dimension, almost like a political revival. Confronted by new human, environmental, economic and social problems, we feel vulnerable. As yesterday's pessimists become the visionaries of tomorrow, design is inevitably carried along by the tide with its

groundswell of naturalism. We feel the need for reassurance and the easy thing is to go back to our roots and trust in nature, even though we are aware that nature may betray us because we have exploited her so cruelly. So our approach is different, less romantic and symbolic than 40 years ago. Today we are threatening our own "home" and flirting with potential disaster. Neo-naturalism picks up on this, embodying the values of a young generation of designers who draw inspiration from the same source as their predecessors but for different reasons. Today they see nature not as a force to be overcome, but as an integral part of their existence. Many of the objects they create result from natural metaphors. Nature is rich not only in forms and outlines, but also in materials and techniques. Anxiety about the environment is increasing and, as always when major changes occur, art forms evolve in parallel. Artists seize hold of the problems, illustrating the new relationships between society and nature by stimulating our collective consciousness. Aesthetic quality is essential in their work, but so is the idea concealed behind it. New spheres of creativity are emerging, based on the theme of nature, and a genuine artistic movement is taking shape.

Giant grass

The Cactus coat stand is part of the I Multipli collection, originally made and distributed by the Italian manufacturer Gufram between the late 1960s and early 1970s. It included very limited runs of functional, everyday objects moulded into the shape of grass or rocks. With key pieces like the Pratone armchair, shaped like a giant clump of grass, by Giorgio Ceretti, Pietro Derossi and Riccardo Rosso, I Multipli is renowned for its offbeat pop vision of naturalism.

Pratone
Collezione I Multipli, Gufram
www.gufram.com

Set in stone

Created in 1968 by designer Piero Gilardi and still in production today, the Sedilsasso is an integral part of Gufram's I Multipli collection. It's a seat, made from grey-lacquered polyurethane to simulate the appearance of a boulder. The rock appears to have shunned its natural environment and come in from the cold to take up residence in the house. The full size version weighs in at 6.5kg, but small and medium sized models are also available. Gather a collection and emulate the natural landscape in the home.

Sassi
Piero Gilardi
www.gufram.com

MYDNA BOOKCASE

IT'S IN THE GENES

MYDNA, pronounced "my DNA", is a novel bookcase dreamt up by Mexican designer Joel Escalona. Twisting up from the floor, the bookcase is reminiscent of the double helix of DNA. The standard model is static, but it's also available in a rotating version that heightens the dynamism of the shape. No wall required – just a suitably stylish collection of books.

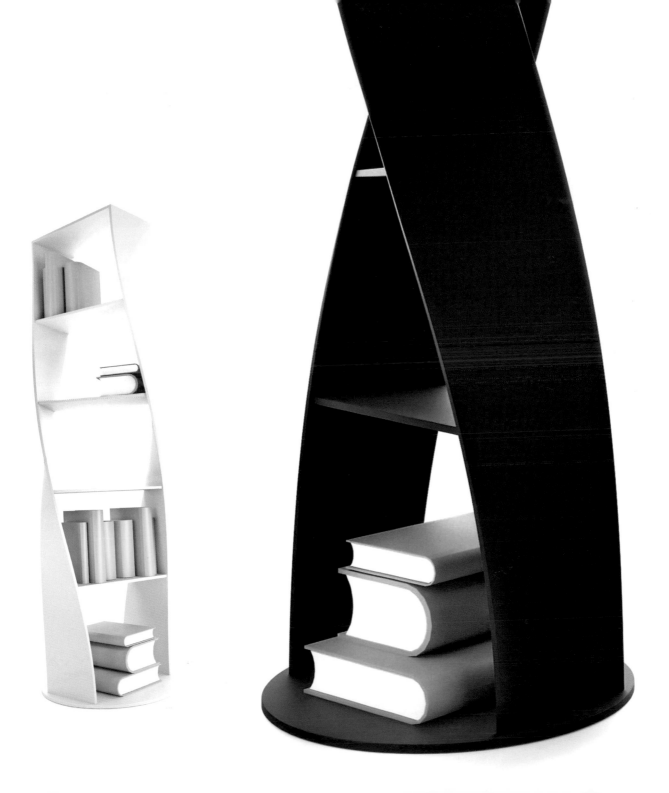

SITTING PRETTY

Fresh from a jewellery collaboration with Louis Vuitton, the artist, producer and N.E.R.D. singer Pharrell Williams has launched his first chair, Perspective, working in tandem with saddler Bruno Domeau and upholsterer Philippe Pérès. Moulded in fibreglass, with leather seats, the chairs are available in four colours, and can be ordered in sets of eight. Whilst highly original, in spirit the Perspective chair also looks back to the style of the 1970s, to the moulded chairs of Charles and Ray Eames and the anthropomorphising of furniture.

.

RUTH FRANKEN'S L'HOMME CHAIR WAS THE ARCHETYPAL EMBODIMENT OF MORPHODESIGN IN 1971; PHARRELL WILLIAMS' CHAIR IS A GOOD EXAMPLE OF WHAT WE THINK OF AS MORPHODESIGN IN 2011.

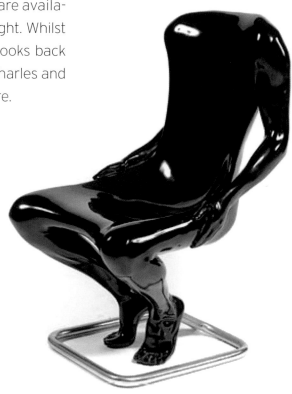

OSSO BUCO

BONE STRUCTURE

Danish designers Ninna Helena Olsen and Lisbeth Hjorslev Toustrup drew inspiration from the organic shapes of *osso buco* (a famous Italian dish but also a term for bone marrow) for a work that blends the functions of a lamp and a seat. The structure of the design reminds us of the way bone and muscle combine, at the same time as playing with space through the use of light. The structure of Osso Buco is supported (appropriately enough) by a spinal column, while illumination comes from three interconnected green or white lamps. Produced by the Hybrido workshop and shown at the Royal Danish Academy of Fine Arts in Copenhagen, Osso Buco responds impressively to the challenge of melding furniture and light with art.

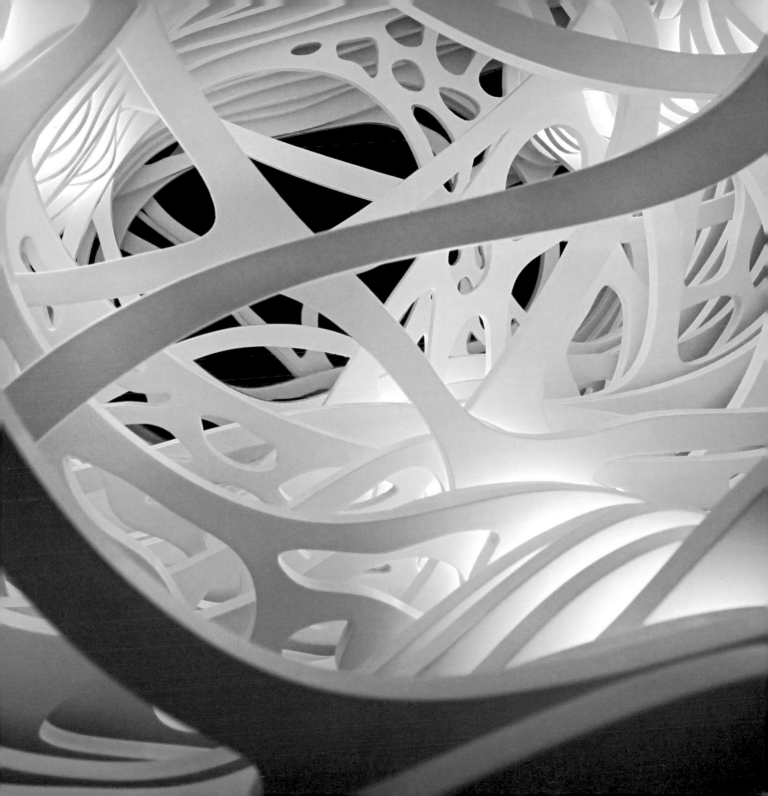

GARDEN HAND

Enzo Berti's garden chair, designed in 2006 and manufactured by Ferlea, tempts you with an invitingly cupped hand. Evocative of the 1960s and the pervading spirit of pop art, the polyethylene chair actually pays greatest homage to the Dada movement, as instigated in 1916 by the Romanian poet Tristan Tzara. The Dadaists elevated the arbitrary and the illogical, rejecting all rational or received ideas. These concepts are reinvigorated here in a chair that evokes the human form with absurd brilliance.

Dimensions: 70cm high, 80cm deep, 65cm wide.
Available in yellow and white.

CLOUD SOFA

REPRODUCE | **D.K. & WEI DESIGN** | www.kootouch.blogspot.com

A CLOUD THAT FLOATS ON HIGH

Ingeniously suspended above the ground, this cloud-shaped seat exudes an air of heavenly tranquillity, as if you yourself might become weightless if you stared at it for long enough. The floating cloud comes from the studios of D. K. & Wei Design. It shares the same design spirit as the Floating Bed, designed by Janjaap Ruijssenaars, founder of Universe Architecture. The technology behind Cloud Sofa is highly innovative: the chair is held in the air by the magnetic force emanating from the base. Alas, you'll have to wait a while before you have the opportunity to sit back and relax on your own Cloud Sofa – at present the chair is still in the virtual stage of production.

HER CHAIR, MAN'S FUTURE?

After being inspired by the Panton Chair, the first injection-moulded plastic chair, created in 1960 by the influential Danish designer Verner Panton, the Italian architect and designer Fabio Novembre said he wanted to "go further," and that "only the human body could make this possible". Reprising Panton's love of curved outlines, the Her Chair emulates the female form using a polyethylene mould. Novembre has a well-established pedigree, having worked for such Italian brands as Cappellini, Driade and Meritalia.

Available in yellow, black, grey, white and brown.

IRONMAN

REPRODUCE SHANE INDER www.i-d.co.nz

PRESSING MATTERS

You've got to wonder why no one has thought of this before. If we're all ironing clothes that fit the human body, why not make an ironing board that fits those clothes? The Ironman is the work of New Zealand designer Shane Inder. Imbued with a sense of intelligence as well as fun, the Ironman's shape means that you can slip a pair of trouser legs over the corresponding limbs on the board for perfect results. The same goes for the wide surface of the board's torso, which is ideal for pressing shirts. A hole in the 'head' accommodates the flex from the iron, reducing the risk of pulling it accidentally off the board. As you might expect, the way in which the Ironman injects colour, humour and heightened practicality into an old, utilitarian object, has attracted plaudits and awards the world over, not least the runner-up prize at the Dyson Awards in 2002.

RECYCLE

The disposable age is on the way out and the days when over-consumption was considered the norm are a thing of the past. Instead, we embrace a new age of sustainable development; an age where waste is ethically unacceptable and recycling becomes a core value. Amid this sea change, slow design is making its mark as a continuing trend. Confronted by the old traditions of standardised, mass-produced objects, designers are coming up with unique or limited-edition goods made from recyclable materials or using traditional techniques. From aircraft-wing desk to pen chandelier, nothing is wasted. Droog Design, the 5.5 Designers collective and Hella Jongerius are leading the way. Ecodesign, slow design, durable design and re-use design – all are emerging from a global movement that fosters changes in behaviour and gives rise to new economic models.

LEFT ON THE SHELF

Werner Aisslinger has mixed recycling and stylish design for the benefit of anyone who collects books or who simply can't bring themselves to throw away old literature. The German designer has created shelving and lamps comprised of interchangeable units that develop and adapt to both the shape of your living space (they work well as room dividers) and the quantity of old books that you have to recycle. Held together by metal rods, the books can be moved around to create the lamp or shelf of your own design. Aisslinger set out to recreate the intimate atmosphere of an old-fashioned bookshop. He succeeds, evoking those times past whilst also looking forward to a new age and all the possibilities that recycling can bring.

THE BIZARRE AND ORIGINAL CREATIONS OF WERNER AISSLINGER, SUCH AS THE TREE LAMP AND THE CORAL SEAT (BELOW), COMBINE INFINITE POSSIBILITIES WITH STYLISH DESIGN.

UNITS OF LIFE

The 90° Furniture system draws on the longstanding relationship between architecture and design. By folding the cardboard units, conceived by Dutch designers Louwrien Kaptein and Menno Bolt, of the Louwrien Kaptein studio, the flat pack can be manipulated into both room partitions and items of furniture. Four units offer different functions: sleeping area, desk, storage space and kitchen. Each unit consists of two flat, jointed panels that open to 90°, and each is composed of cut-out elements that can form desk-tops, work surfaces, shelving, cupboards or seating. With so many different permutations, 90° Furniture not only provides a clever, adaptable means of storing furniture, it also offers a cunning solution to the confines of modern living, defining small, liveable spaces within a larger area.

BATH CHAIR

The Bath & Beyond chair doesn't disguise its humble origins. It's cut straight from a normal bath-tub, with the edges folded to form the arms and a set of steel legs added to bring stability and support. The result is quirky, attractive and surprisingly comfortable. The chair comes from Reddish Studio, a workshop established by Israeli industrial designers Naama Steinbock and Idan Friedman in 2002. Both are graduates of the Holon Academic Institute of Technology, Tel Aviv.

NAAMA STEINBOCK AND IDAN FRIEDMAN ALSO DESIGNED LOUIS 900, A SERIES OF CONTEMPORARY LAMPS THAT UTILISE LEGS RESCUED FROM OLD FURNITURE (TABLES, ARMCHAIRS, ETC.) OF MIXED ORIGIN. ENJOYING THE MINIMALIST WOOD AND ALUMINIUM DESIGN OF THE LAMPS, YOU CAN ONLY SPECULATE ON THE FORMER LIVES OF THEIR CONSTITUENT PARTS.

UNTYRING EFFORTS

Remember the days when an old, unloved tyre looked forward to a retirement spent swinging from a rope under the bough of a tree? These days they're enjoying reinvention as garden chairs that aren't simply functional, but also incorporate a pleasing element of contemporary design. Industrial designer Carl Menary took the worn-out tyre as a starting point for his design, keen to find an environmentally advantageous response to the problems of old, redundant tyres, many of which end up being incinerated (alas, in truth, not enough tyres actually find rejuvenation as garden swings). The Re-Tyre is a model in efficiency; it only takes one salvaged, washed lorry tyre to make a garden chair. Menary simply folds the tyre and fastens it with two bolts. The results are solid, hardwearing and weather resistant, as well as aesthetically pleasing and ecologically sound.

ARE YOU SITTING COMFORTABLY?

The seats in the Softseating series are designed to be used again and again. Constructed partially from recycled kraft paper, the concertina-style structures are stretched out and arranged to form benches, pouffes, divans or tables. Small magnetic panels on the end of each unit enable it to be turned round on itself to form a cylindrical stool or a low table. Each module can also be connected to others of the same size to form long bench seats or sofas. There are as many permutations of shape as there are ways of sitting, stretching or lounging. The paper or non-woven fabric used to make the honeycomb innards softens with age, a process that not only makes the seats increasingly durable and comfortable, but also creates a subtle play of light on the surface. The Softseating structure also gives the seats a remarkable flexibility; each unit can be compressed into a big block and stored on a shelf like a book.

THE PLASTIC CYCLE

Having set themselves the challenge of transforming rubbish into a functional product, English designer Richard Liddle and Cohda Design duly came up with RD Legs. It looks like expertly sculptured tagliatelle, but is, in fact, recycled plastic. Remarkably, the chair is made without using glue. Plastic waste (HDPE, a plastic commonly used in the construction industry, household articles, cars and packaging), which Richard describes as "dead energy", is fed into an extruder, which turns the material into flexible strips. These strips are then arranged on and around a mould by hand whilst still hot. RD Legs, 100% recycled and 100% recyclable, has been acknowledged as important, iconic and environmentally friendly.

GREEN LIGHT

The Grass-On lamp combines and embodies two of the key themes of this book: "Reproduction" and "Recycling". Put simply, it's a cube-shaped lamp covered in fully recyclable synthetic grass. The Grass-On lamp was originally conceived for a charity competition by the Italian designers at ITLab. They were working on new ideas that mixed architecture, design and interior decoration. The result, made entirely from recycled materials, brings the rich lushness of nature into your house. Grass-on can be hung from the ceiling or placed directly on the floor or a table. Several lamps can be placed together, building up larger blocks of greenery. The brightness levels can be adjusted with some simple gardening: to boost the low-intensity light just pull away a little of the vegetation and more light naturally filters through. Any more than that and you might need to reach for the secateurs.

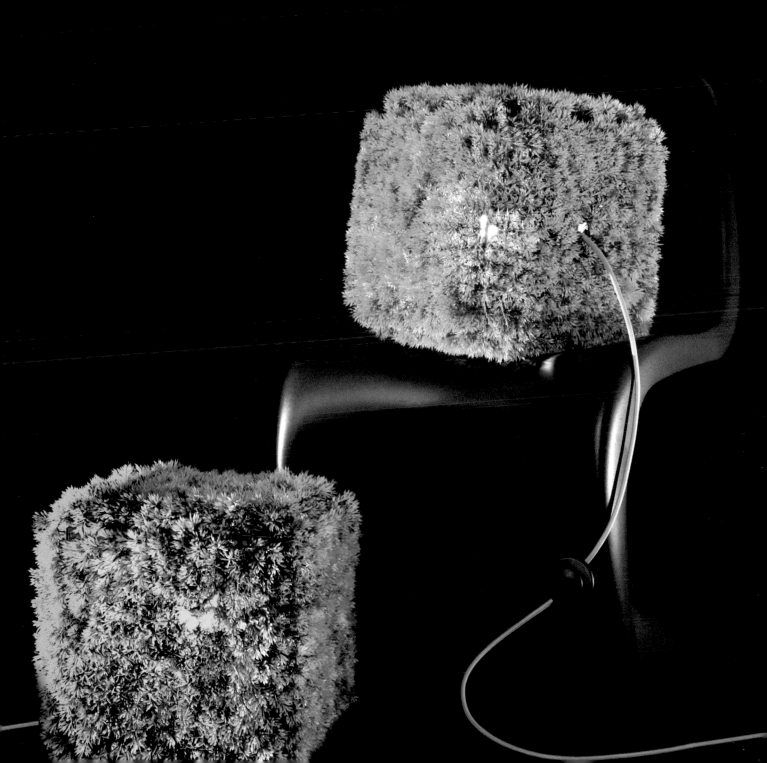

BURIED IN THE GARDEN

This seat with a difference (the difference being you plant it in the garden and let nature do what nature does best) was dreamt up by the fertile minds at the Nucleo design collective. It's a hybrid, eco-friendly chair made, initially, from recycled cardboard. Once you've positioned the skeletal cardboard structure in the garden, cover it with seven wheelbarrow loads of soil and plant some grass seed on the top. Water periodically and within a matter of weeks your luscious green lawn should have an equally luscious green chair positioned in its midst.

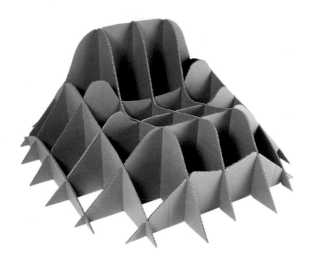

RAGTIME

Rag Chair was first dreamt up by Dutch designer Tejo Remy in 1991. Blending ecological awareness with comfort, the chair comprises successive layers of recycled fabric acquired from the Salvation Army and carefully assembled on a wooden frame. Once positioned, the material is held in place by old packing straps. The limited edition chair is supplied fully formed (and with different fabrics used on every occasion, each chair is, of course, unique), but the manner of its construction enables you to remove and replace fabric as and when the mood takes you, providing a unique way of immortalising an old dress or shirt.

TELLY IN A BOX

The young Dutch designer Christian Kocx has come up with a design-conscious antidote to the flat screen televisions invading homes up and down the land. Use-It Dispose-It draws artful attention to the ecological problems caused by over packaging consumer goods. Kocx has made the packaging a part of the product, encasing the television in a brown, recyclable casket, and buying into the ethos of the slow-design movement in the process. More typically, an old television set and its packaging would be destined for the rubbish tip, but not here. Kocx's enthusiasm and creativity have transformed the items into something new, aesthetically pleasing and ecologically aware.

CLEAR OUT YOUR FILES

Built to a relatively simple design, One Day Paper Waste is a small console table with a shelf. What sets it apart from the norm is the materials used in its construction – the table is built almost entirely from recycled waste paper. Not just any old waste paper either – it all comes (confidential documents included) from one employee at the Lambda Bureau, as collected during the course of a single day. The contents of the employee's waste paper basket were shredded, compressed and then mixed with a transparent vegetable resin. The finished table, designed by Jens Praet and manufactured by Droog Design, is stronger than wood. A glass top puts an attractive head on the intelligent body. Proof, if proof were needed, of the value of recycling.

FLEXIBLE LOVE

CHISHEN CHIU   www.flexiblelove.com

TEST BENCH

Growing family? Don't panic. Flexible Love, created by Taiwanese designer Chishen Chiu, should accommodate your burgeoning brood with room to spare. Like a giant concertina, the cardboard structure (100% recycled, of course) stretches out to form armchair, bench or sofa. Just pull the handle and the seat will grow to a length of seven metres. The inherent bendiness also means that you can sculpt Flexible Love into an arch, a circle, an S or a U, whilst the chair's reinforced honey-comb structure enables you to morph it to the shape of your interior space – curve it round the dinner table if need be. Additionally, that honeycomb composition makes the chair impressively strong – the eight-seater version can support a weight of 960kg; the 16-seater can bear 1720kg. All this strength, all this length and yet, amazingly, Flexible Love folds down to a thickness of just 23.5cm, making it eminently easy to store.

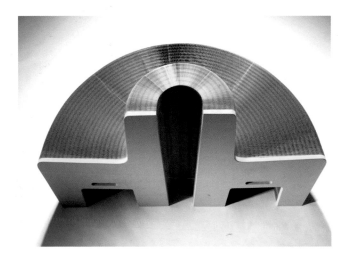

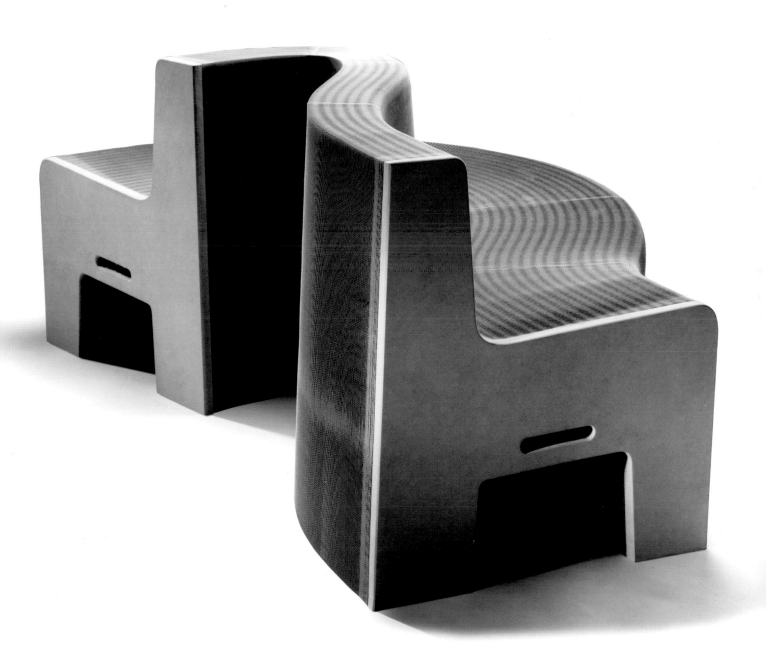

SHOPPING CHAIR

This is Annie, the former supermarket trolley. Past her prime, squeaky and no doubt destined for a canal somewhere in post-industrial Britain, she was rescued by Reestore, a team of English designers headed by Max McMurdo. As you can see, today she's in rude health, reincarnated as an armchair complete with stabilised feet and attractive cushions. Reestore breathe new life into objects headed for the scrapheap by transforming them into accessories or functional furniture. The aim is to avoid using new biomaterials, utilising, instead, any existing materials available. It's an ambition that seems to suit the supermarket trolley particularly well, as an erstwhile symbol of the consumer society, so often found abandoned. Similarly, Reestore have created an aircraft-wing desk, a washing-machine coffee table and a bathtub divan, and are also happy to design objects on request.

PEN CHANDELIER

It's not what you find down the back of the sofa that matters; it's what you do with it afterwards. The Volivik 347 represents an incredible reinvention for the detritus of everyday life, in this instance 347 Bic pens recast as a golden chandelier. Created by the Spanish designers at eStudio enPieza!, the chandelier gathers the biros into four dangling, circular levels, which, once lit, reflect off the walls like a disco ball. You think this is impressive – you should see the large version, a behemoth that makes use of 895 pens!

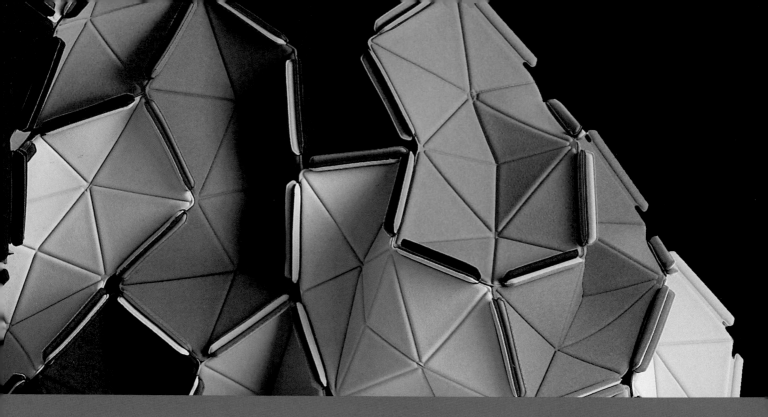

Designers have begun to rewrite the rules for certain objects. They come up with stackable, haphazard, variable structures that function as tables one minute and divans the next. They like playing with Lego® as well as building life-size constructions, maintaining the childish simplicity that can be so refreshing and inventive in design. Nevertheless, their creations involve genuine technical and conceptual innovation, whilst the objects or items of furniture can usher in new habits and new ways of living. In common, these designers "dare" to revitalise our everyday existence, and they do it with no small degree of humour. Equally, the same designers never lose sight of functionality – preserving the function of everyday objects, even while they bring us innovative, pioneering design.

SPECTRE

ANTENNA DESIGN

www.antennadesign.com

SHIFTING SAND

Created for the World Design Capital 2008 in Turin, Spectre invites us to reconstruct our interior spaces, to constantly make and undo, spawning barricades, sofas, carpets or armchairs. The name is an acronym – Special Environment for Childplay Teamwork Regression and Entertainment – assigned to highlight the combination of practicality and fun at work in the product. It's a design with multiple coloured parts, each a bag filled with sand. Spectre originates with the Antenna Design collective, set up in 1997 by Masamichi Udagawa and Sigi Mœslinger to make products with original, interchangeable and sometimes childish designs.

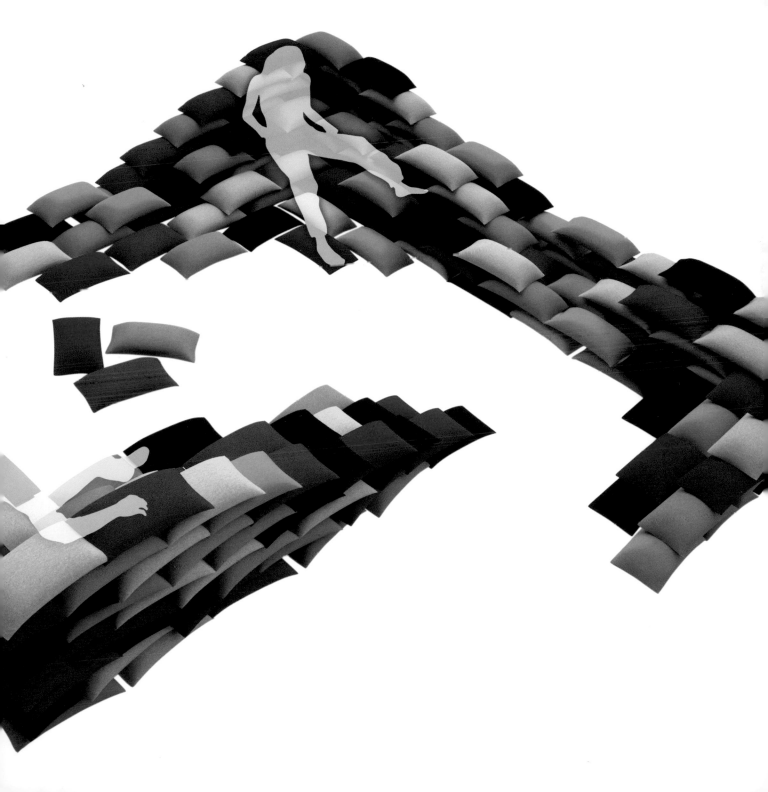

MÖVENPICK ICE LOUNGE

CLAUDIO COLUCCI   www.colucci-design.com

LOUNGE AROUND

You can kind of gauge how much the good folk at Mövenpick value their ice cream by the importance they attach to how and where you eat it. They've turned it into a full-blown event. The Mövenpick Ice Lounge is a cocoon-shaped paean to the cold stuff; its forms and colouring (white lacquer with a tinge of pink) distinctly reminiscent of an ice cream scoop. It's the work of Claudio Colucci, inspired by a piece of empire style furniture known as a conversation sofa. "This creation," he explains, "is conceived as a multi-sensory sphere, the materialisation of a perpetual motion, like a rising scroll, the sign of lightness and sweetness."

CLAUDIO COLUCCI IS AN INTERIOR ARCHITECT, DESIGNER AND STAGE DESIGNER WITH A NUMBER OF STRINGS TO HIS BOW. HE DIVIDES HIS TIME BETWEEN PARIS AND TOKYO AND ALTERNATES BETWEEN DESIGNING INTERIORS (SUCH AS THE HÔTEL LUMEN NEAR THE LOUVRE) AND CREATING BEAUTIFUL OBJECTS - WITNESS THE PLATE HE CREATED SPECIALLY FOR THE CHEF ALAIN PASSARD.

OPEN, SESAME!

The speed at which books can pile up in the house always comes as a surprise. Before you know it you need new shelves to accommodate your books, and before too long a bigger house to accommodate those shelves. The ingenious Rek Bookcase, brainchild of Dutch designer Reinier de Jong, can help you keep up with your book collection, growing (or contracting) to fit the number of books and the available room space. In its dormant, folded state, the bookcase compacts, its five staggered elements slotting neatly together. To open the shelving, simply pull the two ends apart, thereby opening up the space for books in between. The Rek Bookcase is available in several Pantone colours.

BROTHERLY LOVE

The Bouroullec brothers have been revolutionising international design for the last decade, carving a reputation for unmissable and influential work. Despite their relative youthfulness – Ronan was born in 1971 and Erwan in 1976 – the brothers, of Breton farming stock, have won widespread recognition, enjoying full-page spreads in the Herald Tribune, patronage from the MOMA and the Pompidou Centre, and an exhibition at the Design Museum in London. The brothers went into partnership in 1999. Ronan had completed his studies at the École Nationale des Arts Décoratifs and, after a short period working alone, was joined by Erwan, then still a student at the École des Beaux-Arts in Cergy-Pontoise.

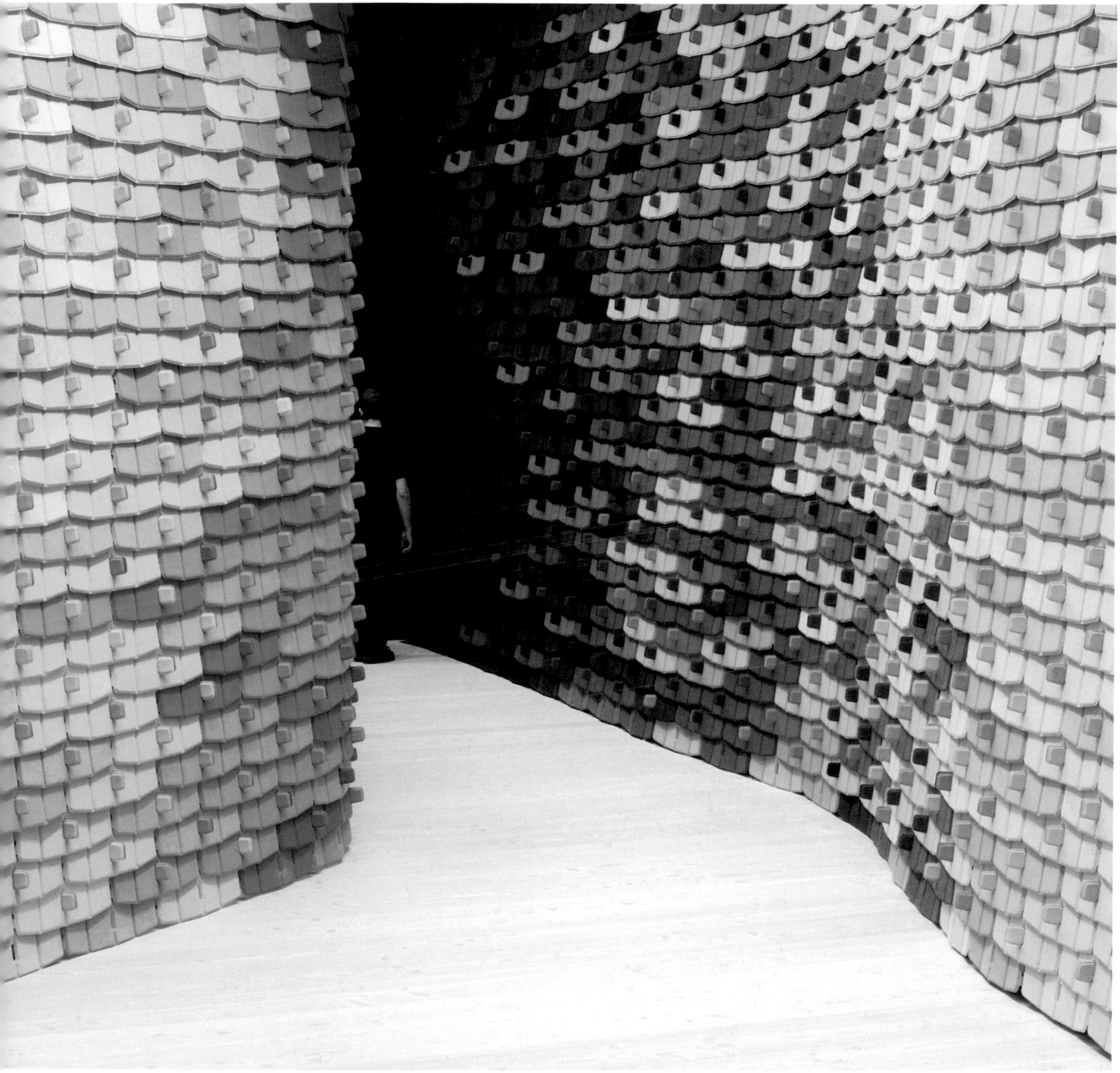

They tapped into the spirit of the times, reinventing furniture with brilliant new ideas. Success came quickly, and the big companies, including Vitra, Kartell, Cappellini, Ligne-Roset, Habitat and the Galerie Kréo, lined up to manufacture the brothers' work. From the Tapis à Fermeture Éclair® to the Cuisine Désintégrée, via the Vase Combinatoire and the divan enclosed in a black box, their designs have shaken our habits and conventions.

The Bouroullecs play creative ping-pong, firing ideas back and forth, driving each other into corners until, at the end of a complex process, they arrive at the perfect object. They are interdependent, complementary and symbiotic, the right and left-hand pushing back the boundaries of creation, consistently progressive yet always natural. Intuitively, they come up with delicately poetic, elegantly simple designs. Constantly seeking new applications developed from a minimum of materials, they employ a modular approach to design, piecing elements together and redefining space. And yet, as radical as all that sounds, throughout, they pursue the ideas of comfort and usefulness. In little over ten years the Bouroullec brothers and their fun yet functional products have become true icons of design.

Head in the clouds

Designed for Kvadrat in 2009, the multicoloured cloud works on the same principle as the tiles. It is composed of multiple fabric modules, which can be linked together to form infinite different patterns and arrangements. Clips are used to fasten the elements in place, and the whole can then be hung on the wall or from the ceiling. Each minor rearrangement of the tiles changes the complexion of the cloud. The infinitely variable cloud can be used as a colourful room divider, a three-dimensional wall hanging or simply as an amorphous, highly unusual object of visual interest.

Clouds
www.bouroullec.com

Interactive and adaptable

There's a consistent, navigable creative thread running through the Bouroullecs' work; each design follows a certain logic that's inspired by the last work and looks forward to the next. This continuous narrative emerges again in the Grape rug, manufactured by the Galerie Kréo in 2001. Each "bunch of grapes" is made up of twelve circles, 30cm in diameter, which are sewn together. The result is a pared down, fun rug with a delightfully minimalist spirit. Each rug, produced by one of the famed Aubusson factories, is made from 100% Woolmark wool velour, and comes in shades of blue and grey. Like much of the Bouroullecs' design, the interactive element to the Grape carpet allows you to move and place the components into whatever arrangement you prefer.

Grape carpet
www.bouroullec.com

A place for everything

The Joyn office, manufactured by Vitra in 2002, is an open system promoting alternative ways of working. Whether you work individually or as part of a team, the system encourages communication and facilitates interaction by removing the physical barriers between individuals. The design features moveable storage spaces, adjustable partitions and 'micro-architecture', allowing the users to reinvent the office space specifically for the demands of the latest project, whether that requires group working or time spent individually focussed on particular tasks. Joyn was inspired by the traditional farmhouse table, the brothers drawing on memories of their grandparents' farm to find ways of reinventing the communal, multi-purpose hub.

Joyn office system
www.bouroullec.com

Green wave

Playing once more on the traditional methods of space division, the Bouroullec brothers came up with the idea of seaweed as a physical boundary. Not real seaweed of course, but injection-moulded plastic-effect seaweed, as manufactured for the brothers by Vitra. The 'plants' can be linked together to form woven structures, varying from a thin, open curtain to an impenetrable green hedge. Urbanites longing for the unspoiled greenery of the natural world can reconstitute a tangle of vegetation in the home and adjust it as they please. The Bouroullecs' seaweed can be seen amongst the collections at the MOMA in New York.

Algues
www.bouroullec.com

Mobile cabin

Did the Bouroullec brothers' Breton origins inspire the contemporary box bed? Designed in 2000 and manufactured by the Galerie Kréo, the sleeping cabin – already a cult object – sums up their design philosophy. Bigger than a bed and smaller than a bedroom, the box is closed-off enough to preserve privacy and yet, at the same time, open enough to negate any sense of claustrophobia. It consists of a base made of two trestles and a cabin covered in wire mesh, with a sliding door of painted wood and a plastic window. The mobile cabin lives up to its name – the whole thing can be moved around the house as your wanderlust dictates.

Lit Clos
www.bouroullec.com

A QUIET READ

Reading is a solitary pleasure, one of those activities that simply demand peace and quiet for adequate concentration. However, finding a tranquil niche in which to cosy up with a good book isn't that easy in the modern world. The Cave bookcase offers a snug retreat from the hustle and bustle, its clever design enabling the reader to become literally ensconced in their books – it's a real Ali Baba's cave right in the middle of the bookcase. Like most moveable bookcases, the Cave also functions very well as an attractive room divider. It's the work of Sakura Adachi, a Japanese designer resident in Italy. Two versions are available – one for children, the other for adults.

THE CAVE BOOKCASE ALSO COMES IN A VERSION FOR ANIMALS. WHO SAYS DOGS DON'T NEED PRIVACY WHEN SETTLING DOWN TO A GOOD BOOK?

FOLDING AND UNFOLDING

This discreet, elegant stool is reminiscent of a helix. Constructed without screws and with no axle, it folds and unfolds in a highly unusual way. The Oneshot is all about the vertical axis – pick it up and it looks floppy and unable to support the lightest weight, but stand it up, apply pressure from above and the structure locks into place, using gravitational force to create a strong platform on which to sit. Once folded, the Oneshot also takes up less space than its conventional cousins.

PATRICK JOUIN IS AN EMBLEMATIC FIGURE OF CONTEMPORARY DESIGN. A FORMER ASSOCIATE OF PHILIPPE STARCK, HE NOW WORKS INDEPENDENTLY AND HAS EXPANDED INTO NEW AREAS OF ACTIVITY. THOUGH PATRICK HAS DESIGNED INTERIORS, SUCH AS THE RESTAURANT JULES VERNE IN THE EIFFEL TOWER, HE STILL PREFERS DREAMS AND PLAY, AS CAN BE SEEN FROM HIS TARTINUTELLA, A SPATULA DESIGNED ESPECIALLY FOR SPREADING NUTELLA®.

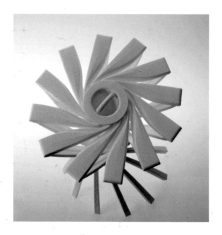

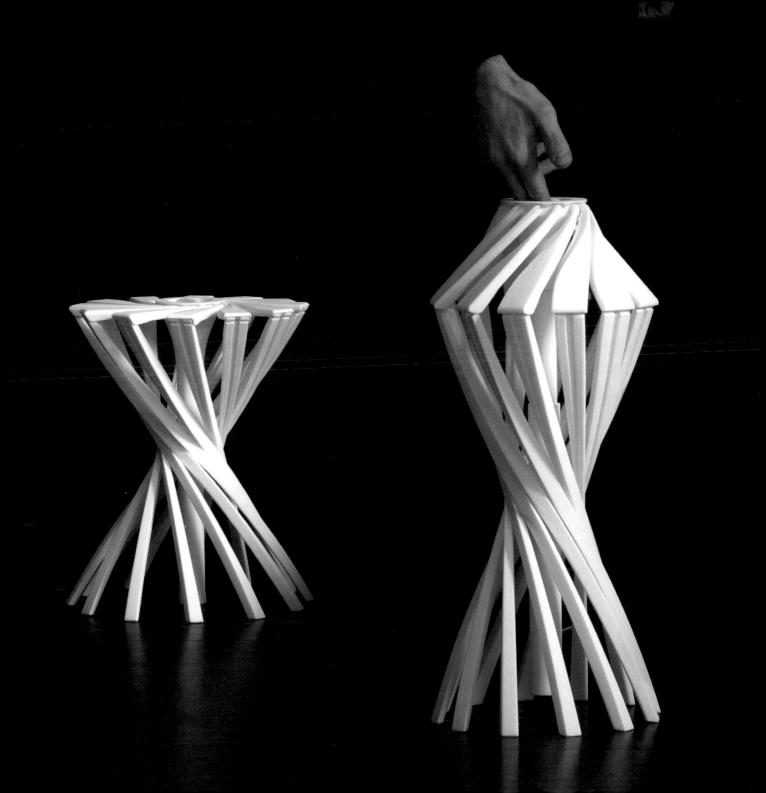

INTELLIGENT HASSOCK

Harsha Vardhan R's hassock is a remarkable piece of design. Concealed within this modern looking pouffe is a fully functioning washing machine. Remarkable enough in itself, but throw in the fact that the washing machine doesn't use any water, and the kudos for Harsha grows further. The machine uses ionised air, capable of cleaning all kinds of textiles. Where can you get one? At the moment you can't – Harsha is still working on the designs. Watch this space, as they say.

POSSIBLE FURNITURE

CONSTRUCTION SET

Fed up with your shabby old furniture, just sitting there, large and immobile? Possible Furniture represents a versatile, modern alternative. Comprised of multiple moveable elements, the furniture is at your beck and call, to be reshaped or moved as the need arises. The components, shaped like large smooth tablets, are made from fabric, foam and lacquered wood. They can be piled high to make a writing desk or kept low to shape a daybed. Possible Furniture combines originality and practicality: the stability and durability being backed up with simple, sleek aesthetics.

ROBERT STADLER HAS WORKED FOR WELL-KNOWN BRANDS SUCH AS DIOR AND ORANGE. WITH POSSIBLE FURNITURE, HE CLOUDS THE DISTINCTION BETWEEN DESIGN AND CONTEMPORARY ART AS HE DELVES MORE DEEPLY INTO THE ROLE OF THE CREATOR.

FEELING YOUR WAY

Reworking the classics is a key ambition of contemporary design. By inventing new uses for existing objects, we can see how creativity responds to functional logic. Here's a fine example: Hong Kong-based designer Zhiliang Chen has transformed the well-known Rubik's Cube in six colours into a tactile Rubik's Cube for blind people. The colours are replaced by easily identified materials, creating surfaces of wood, fabric, stone and rubber. Not that any of this makes actually solving the Rubik's Cube any easier...

ON YOUR KNEES

Ah, the simple pleasures of a cuppa. Nothing beats a tea or a coffee in the middle of the afternoon, whether you're lounging in front of the television or curled up on the sofa with a good book. The only problem is the attendant paraphernalia, not least the coasters and a coffee table on which to rest your steaming brew. The Knee Mug from the Thelermont Hupton collective appears to offer an easy solution. In their quest to make everyday life more pleasant, David Hupton and Yve Thelermont have come up with a simple, obvious and brilliant device: a mug that sits comfortably on the knee. The earthenware mugs are available in several colours.

THIS PARTICULAR COLLECTION ALSO FEATURES LAP MUGS AND BEST EVERYDAY CUPS, ALL ADAPTED TO FIT THOSE MODERN DAY HABITS. ANOTHER DESIGN, THE THUMB BOWL PLATE, FEATURES A HOLE IN THE MIDDLE FOR EASE OF HOLDING.

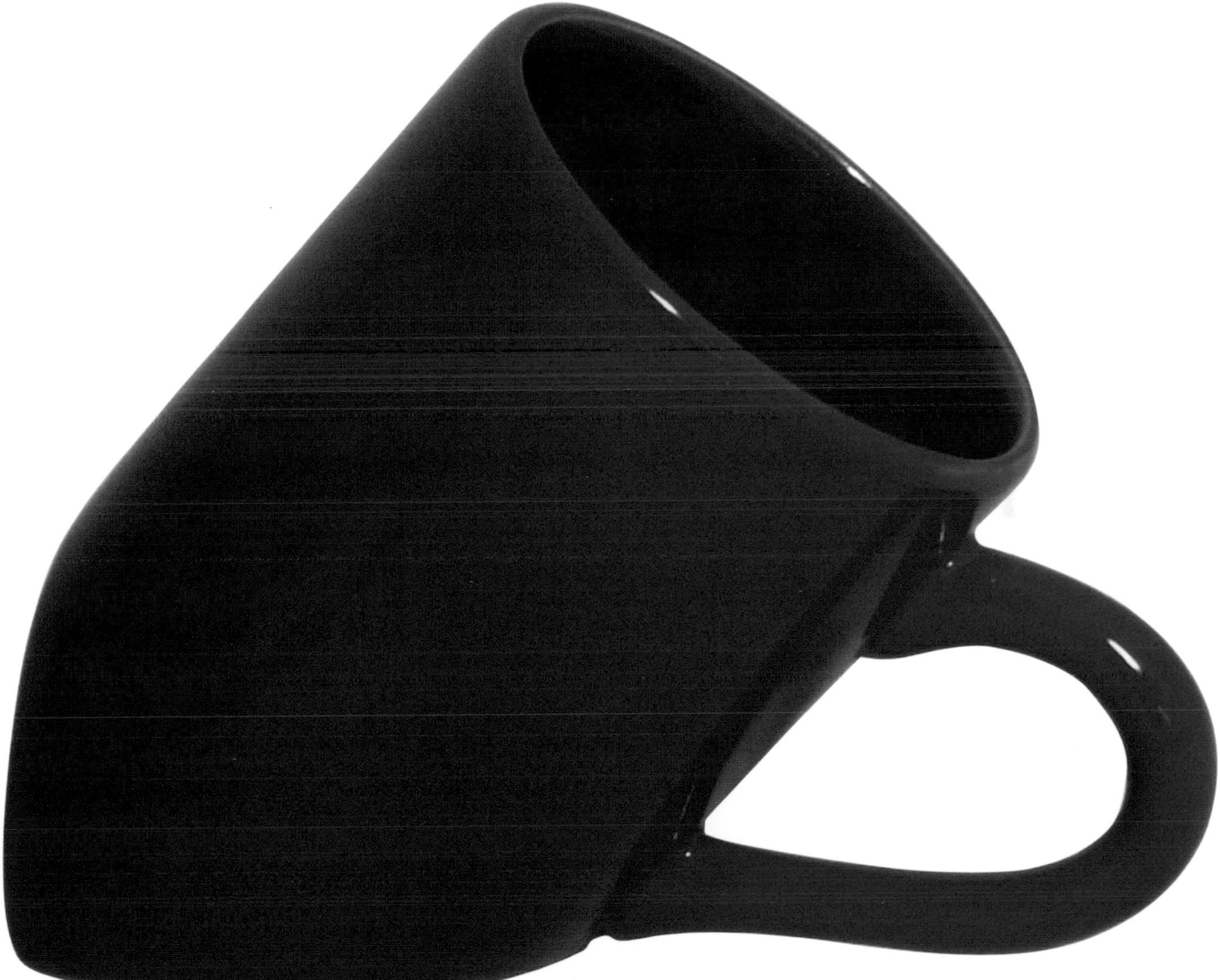

THE CHAIR

HYUH JIN LEE & HYEROUNG CHOEN www.hyuhjinlee.com

HANG IT ALL!

Finding somewhere to put your handbag in a restaurant isn't as easy as it should be. On the floor it's in danger of being trampled, on the table it gets in the way and on the spare chair, hogging an entire seat to itself, the bag draws dirty looks from other diners. The Chair, created by Korean designer Hyuh Jin Lee, provides a practical, elegant solution. At first glance it looks like the understated white chair has acquired antlers, but closer inspection reveals the growth to be a bag, hat or scarf stand. Minimalist, practical and attractive – The Chair is a masterpiece of modern design.

THE CONCEPT OF THE COAT-STAND CHAIR HAS OCCUPIED MORE THAN ONE DESIGNER IN RECENT YEARS. ASIDE FROM HYUH JIN LEE'S EXAMPLE, YOU MIGHT ALSO HAVE NOTICED CREATIONS LIKE THE TREE CHAIRS BY DAVID ROBERT OR CHRISTIAN VIVANCO.

TABLE MANNERS

When Marc Ligos designed the Conclusion No. 7: Table, his main aim was to make anyone using the table more aware of their relationship with furniture and with objects in general. And, when you have to support the weight of the table on your legs for it to actually serve as a table, you'd have to say that Ligos has achieved his ambition. The exaggerated interaction between person and table perhaps shows that objects lack any meaning unless they're being used. Even if you don't buy into the theory, thinking about it will at least draw your attention away from the growing numbness in your legs...

THINKING ABOUT THE NECESSITY OF OBJECTS IS MARC LIGOS'S FAVOURITE SUBJECT, AS EVIDENCED BY SEVERAL OF HIS DESIGNS. TAKE, FOR EXAMPLE, THE CHAIR WITH TWO LEGS THAT ONLY STANDS UP IF YOU SIT ON IT, OR THE GLASS THAT YOU CAN ONLY FILL BY BLOCKING THE HOLES IN THE SIDES WITH YOUR FINGERS.

THROUGH THE LOOKING GLASS

If you find shopping a bore, this design from architect Siebe Tettero and SZI Design might just make the experience more interesting. It's a mad hybrid of maze and wonderland; an offbeat store that reinvents the rules of shopping with its upside down layout. Viktor Horsting and Rolf Snœren (aka Viktor & Rolf) also worked on the design, turning mirrors and handles around the wrong way, gluing chairs to the ceiling and chandeliers to the floor. Perhaps the disorientation was just too much – the shop, originally in Milan, has been closed since 2008. Here's hoping it reopens some time soon.

INTERIOR DESIGN IS ATTRACTING MORE AND MORE CREATIVE ARTISTS, EAGER TO USE THEIR SKILLS IN THE SERVICE OF TRENDY BOUTIQUES, BARS, RESTAURANTS AND SHOWROOMS. FABIO NOVEMBRE, PHILIPPE STARCK, MARCEL WANDERS AND MATALI CRASSET, NOT TO MENTION MARTÍ GUIXÉ, HAVE ALREADY JOINED IN THE FUN.

DREAM

This chapter brings together a selection of pieces, from vegetable shoes to a tree trunk bench, that will leave you speechless, amazed, delighted and transfixed by their audacity, their sturdiness or their beauty. Exceptional, hybrid, mutant, dreamlike and offbeat, these objects rewrite the rulebook, overturning accepted practice to shake your long-held convictions. Many result from a fusion of design and contemporary art; a marriage that generates

Dream: give free rein to your imagination, become absorbed in your wishes and desires.

iconoclastic work, some of it spectacular and sophisticated, some of it subtle and discreet, but all of it stylish and sensual. Make room in your life for a little dreaming.

MUTANT VASES

Cédric Ragot defies classification. A born innovator, this versatile young designer breaks new ground through the use of materials and shapes, yet upholds the well-established traditions of industrial design. His résumé grows apace: he first caught the public's attention with a 'mutant' stool called La Chose (The Thing), and has subsequently cemented his reputation with the Liquid Mobile Phone, with boots created for Puma and via furniture designed for Cappellini and Roche Bobois. Here, the series of Fast Vases has the feeling of a hybrid, caught somewhere between stasis and rapid movement. They're frozen in the process of acceleration, appearing to be on the move yet static in the midst of dynamic motion.

THE FAST VASES WERE FIRST PRODUCED IN 2003. IN 2007 THEY RECEIVED A GOOD DESIGN AWARD FROM THE CHICAGO ATHENAEUM (MUSEUM OF ARCHITECTURE AND DESIGN), AND WERE MARKETED BY ROSENTHAL. THEY WERE ALSO PRODUCED IN BLACK.

TREE TRUNK BENCH

TRUNK CALL

How do we remain a part of the natural world in this, the consumerist age? It's a question that inspired Dutch designer Jurgen Bey to create the Tree Trunk Bench. Indeed, the question is writ large in the product itself. He began with the simple (and it must be said, wholly unoriginal) observation that a fallen tree trunk can be used as seating. By adding a bronze chair back he developed the fallen log into something much more suggestive of 'developed' furniture – culture and nature in harmony said the plaudits. And then Jurgen insisted that, because it is ridiculous to transport the trees around when there's probably a perfectly good one available locally, only the chair backs are for sale.

SEISMIC SHOCK

The Esquire Rug, designed for Top Floor by Esti Barnes, won the British Design of the Year Award in 2008. You can see why: the originality of the design, the inherent style and the beguiling realism (it feels like walking across a patterned Sahara, or even the surface of Mars made decorative by meticulous aliens) make it an instant design classic. Made of wool, the rug comes in several colours and various sizes. Esti has built her reputation on rugs, each with its own intriguing design. Even the names are evocative: Emphasis, Ethereal, Envelope, Equator and even Etna! In common, Esti's rugs usually focus on material and shape, whether that's granular, in relief, with waves or cut outs, or even with folded paper mixed in (see opposite).

ETHEREAL, THE SECOND RUG COMMISSIONED BY TOP FLOOR, HAS BAROQUE
ORNAMENTATION WITH FLORAL MOTIFS AT THE ENDS.

THESE BOOTS WEREN'T MADE FOR WALKING

Wafting temptation under the noses of shoe lovers, photographer Michel Tcherevkoff brings us footwear that is just too good to actually use. Even if you did try walking in the Shoe Fleur collection you wouldn't get very far — each design has been sculpted by Michel from a single variety of flower, leaf or plant. One pair is composed from thistles; another is made from white lilies; a third from bicoloured orchids, banana leaves or huge, exotic beans. All manner of footwear, from platforms to stilettos, boots to sandals, is represented in the extraordinary, ephemeral collection. The delicacy and artistry of the shoes is only heightened by their inevitably short lifespan.

THE 75 FLORAL SHOES OF THE COLLECTION ARE GROUPED BY SEASON IN THE BOOK *SHOE FLEUR*, PUBLISHED BY WELCOME BOOKS.

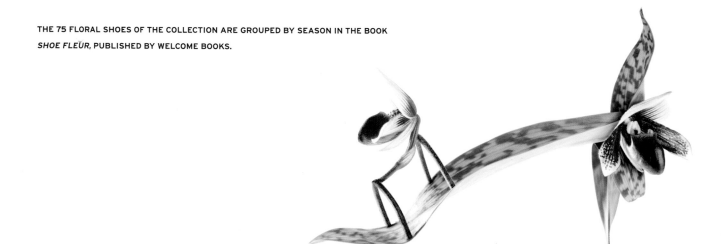

BETWEEN DESIGN AND ART

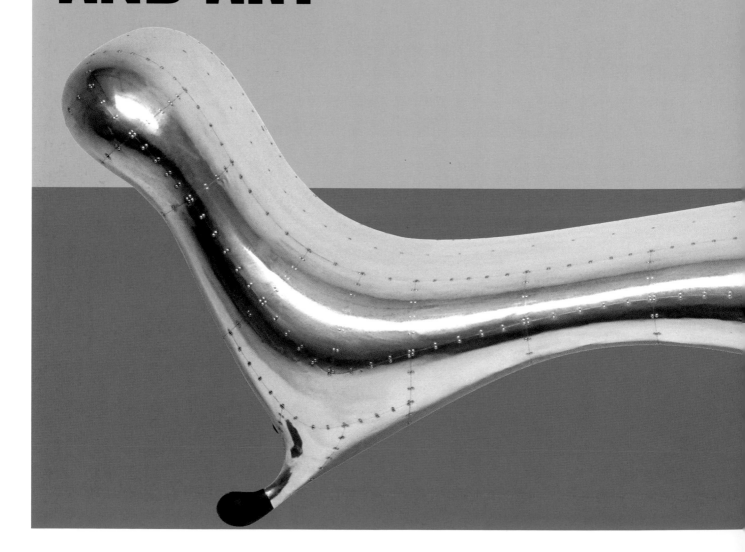

Design is "a creative activity that determines the formal qualities of industrially manufactured objects". Sometimes this meeting of art and industry is deliberately pushed off balance. Design can give us access to the highest level of abstraction, and almost becomes a work of art in itself, disguised only by the fact that it retains some vestige of functionality. Certain designers position themselves half way between industrial design and art. They retain that interest in functionality, but also embrace the beauty of objects, of dematerialising and abstraction, as in the theory of art for art's sake, of beauty and of aestheticism.

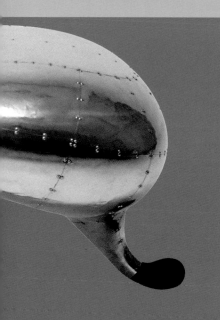

All-time record

Recently auctioned in London for the modest sum of £1,000,000, the Lockheed Lounge chaise longue has become an icon of design. Created by Marc Newson in 1986, the chair fluctuates between purity of form and dynamic lines. Newson, an ardent enthusiast for new materials, used carbon fibre, steel and composite materials to make the Lockheed Lounge. There is only one of these out there, a fact that has added to the object's status and billing as a 'work of art'. But the biggest impression has been made, undeniably, by the Lockheed Lounge's price. As for Newson, his reputation grows and grows; witness the recent exhibition of his work organised by the famous American gallery owner Larry Gagosian.

Lockheed Lounge
Marc Newson
www.marc-newson.com

Futuristic pipework

Zaha Hadid is famous throughout the world as an architect, but she also gets highly involved in conceiving and designing objects. She creates futuristic, abstract designs that often hide or obscure (without negating) the object's function. For example, the fluid lines and refinement of the tap she designed for Triflow make it more work of art than bathroom fitting. State-of-the-art technology inside the tap filters the water as it passes through, and even warns the user when the filter needs changing.

Avilion Triflow
Zaha Hadid
www.zaha-hadid.com

Convolutions

The emblematic Israeli designer Ron Arad works with new technologies and innovative materials. Developing his taste for curves, he creates like a sculptor. Voido, a seat with refined, dynamic lines, shows off Arad's predilection for the processes of transformation, manipulation and experimentation.

Voido
Ron Arad
www.ronarad.com

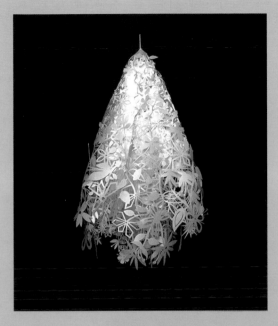

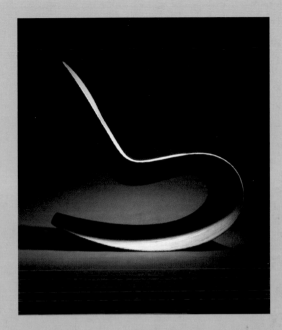

Fairytale world

The terms "elegance" and "poetry" could both be used to describe the work of Tord Boontje. Combining traditional craft techniques with new technologies, his style wavers between what he describes as "the romantic and the technological". In particular, Boontje has used his talents for designing lamps, including the Blossom chandelier created in 2002 for Swarovski, a branch of cut-glass flowers adorned with LED lamps and controlled by computer, and also Little Field of Flowers, the famous carpet of red autumn leaves that met with enormous success.

Blossom
Tord Boontje
www.tordboontje.com

A perfect line

A chair blessed with pure lines, the wooden Savannah Rocker, from the ODE Chair collection, is modelled on the famous Panton chair. It's an everyday object for which refinement and beauty have come to rival functionality. The designer, Jolyon Yates, offers a wide range of chairs, each one more elegant than the last. The rocking chair version of the ODE Chair (shown above) is made of beechwood.

Savannah Rocker
Jolyon Yates
www.jolyonyates.com

PILE THEM HIGH

David Pier's Ultimate Coffee Cups blend beauty with practicality. The curved asymmetry brings a new visual edge to the mundanity of an everyday object, whilst the ingenious shaping of the handle and rim fit the cups perfectly to hand and mouth. Additionally, the form of the cup and saucer make them easy and interesting to stack (when was the last time you heard that said about coffee cups?). David sums up the approach himself: "Beautiful and original in appearance and superior at the functional level."

LESS LAMP

CUSTOMISE YOUR LAMP

Tapping a lamp with a hammer usually has fairly predictable results, and, as a consequence, few of us attempt it on a regular basis. How refreshing then, to be positively encouraged to take the hammer in hand to work on this, the Less Lamp, the light that wants you to tap away. Created by Spanish designer Jordi Canudas, the Less Lamp has been designed to reveal a little more light every time you give it a gentle tap. You begin with the opaque black or white lamp and create a unique piece with the design of your choice, varying the intensity of the light with every tap of the hammer. A word of warning – don't go hell for leather, even the Less Lamp has its breaking point.

THE LAMPS ARE MANUFACTURED BY METALARTE AND COME IN BLACK OR WHITE.
THEY RECENTLY FOUND THEIR WAY INTO THE PERMANENT COLLECTION AT THE MOMA.

THIS IS NOT A PIPE

Jeremy Brown has subverted the original functions of the objects in his collection of glasses and mugs. He's taken inspiration from René Magritte, the Belgian surrealist who famously wrote "This is not a pipe" on one of his paintings. In the same vein, Jeremy Brown loudly declares, "This is (not)" a cup. He explores the theory on the "treachery of images", creating mugs with six handles or wineglasses that look more like soup plates, all of it designed to mess with our assumptions. Inevitably, we are distracted from the original function of the objects into considering them as something less prosaic.

VERSATILE AND CREATIVE, JEREMY BROWN WORKS IN LONDON. THE INFLUENTIAL MAGAZINE *WALLPAPER* RECENTLY WROTE OF HIM AS A MEMBER OF THE "NEXT GENERATION OF DESIGNERS". HIS WORK CAN BE BOUGHT ON HIS WEBSITE.

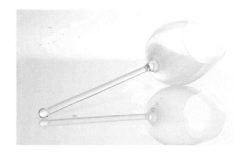 

WET PAINT

Hovering somewhere between design object and work of art, the dripping table, imploringly entitled Paint or Die but Love Me, was created by the young French designer John Nouanesing. It's like trompe l'oeil in 3D, the metal sheet of the tabletop apparently floating in space with the contents of a can of red paint tipped all over its surface and dripping down onto the floor. What looks like viscous red paint is actually steel covered in glossy acrylic, cleverly manipulated to form the legs of the table.

AFTER THE LIQUID LAMP AND THE LIQUID BOOKMARK BY THE JAPANESE COLLECTIVE KYOUEI DESIGN,
PAINT OR DIE BUT LOVE ME OFFERS US ANOTHER ORIGINAL AND STYLISH CREATION THAT ATTEMPTS
TO REPRODUCE THE FLOW OF LIQUID.

PALIMPSEST LAMPSHADE

The devil finds large interactive lampshades for idle hands... as the saying doesn't go. Un Peu, Beaucoup, a light designed by French collective L'Air de Rien, is designed so that you can pull off bits of white paper to give the shade a continually evolving appearance. Each leaf removed from the white cover reveals new colours and varies the intensity of the light. Several layers of differently coloured paper allow those idle hands ample chance to get busy, shaping new motifs every time they do.

un peu

beaucoup

un peu, beaucoup . . .

MUSICAL CHAIRS

Visit Ante Vojnovic's website and you'll find chairs that move to the sound of the tango in languorous, slightly surreal dance. Once again, we find functionality matched move for move by absorbing design, encouraging us to rethink those old perceptions. Tango Variations rejects normal values, stylishly subverting what we traditionally think of as a chair. Hollow backed and warped, the chairs have lightweight legs and uncomfortable seats. But that's not the point! Ante's description of himself as a "mystical artist, busy looking at things that don't exist," might help explain where he's coming from. Or not...

TANGO VARIATIONS BROUGHT ANTE VOJNOVIC THE OPPORTUNITY TO EXHIBIT AT THE AOSANDO TRADE FAIR IN TOKYO IN 2008. THE DESIGNER AND ARTIST, WHO LIVES IN JAPAN, IS MUCH ADMIRED FOR THE PURITY AND ORIGINALITY OF HIS WORK.

SPECIAL FRAGRANCE

Matali Crasset's offbeat and original creations are often imbued with poetry, lightness and delicacy. She ventures beyond the simple creation of objects into the realms of interior decoration, furniture and artistic installation, approaching her task from an unashamedly artistic perspective. Sunic (see opposite), a perfume holder in which the fragrance appears suspended bulbously in space, was created for the Gandy Gallery in Prague in 2002. Inspired by light, the fluidity of contrasts and the play of shapes, it can be hung up like a lamp, displayed like a sculpture or stood directly on top of a piece of furniture. Matali also created a special fragrance for Sunic, which can be used to scent a room or as an eau de parfum.

IN 2009, MATALI CRASSET EXHIBITED SOME OF HER CREATIONS AT THE GALERIE ART CURIAL IN PARIS. THESE INCLUDED IN VINO VERITAS: DIFFERENT CONTAINERS ASSOCIATED WITH WINE AND WINE TASTING, SUCH AS MOUTH-BLOWN BOTTLES AND CARAFES MADE IN THE CZECH REPUBLIC.

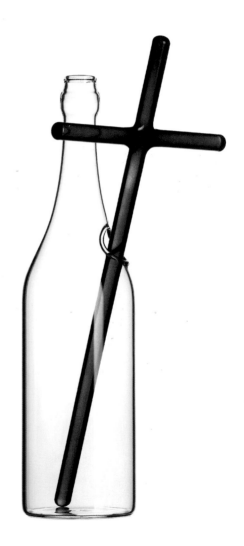

WALLFLOWERS

Swedish textile designer Hanna Nyman created 3D Wallpaper to brighten up gloomy interiors. The paper comes inlaid with a variety of designs, which can be peeled off to reveal different patterns – the residual paper hanging out from the wall gives the design its 3D element. Pick off as little or as much as you like. Inspired by the shapes and techniques of origami, Hanna's 3D Wallpaper is progressive, hands-on, unexpected and constantly evolving; its roots planted more in narrative than functionality.

**THIS WALLPAPER WAS ON SHOW AT THE EXHIBITION "A WORLD OF FOLK"
IN NORWAY, BUT IS NOT YET ON SALE.**

LACED UP

Marcel Wanders' absorbing and original creations bear witness to his research into the relationship between material and form. His work utilises traditional materials in a modern way to generate contemporary design. Crocheted fibres, set in epoxy resin and then remodelled, give the chairs their shape. The chair pictured opposite, Crochet Chair and Solid White, was exhibited at Smart Deco in Miami in 2006, but Wanders first caught our attention with Knotted Chair, a work made in macramé and with a simple, almost vintage form. His Carbon Chair followed a similar approach, achieving an equal measure of light, airy inventiveness.

TRAVELLING LIGHT

Reminiscent of the complex amalgam found in a chain of molecules, this amazing light has the ability to move and reinvent itself. The polymorphic, modular structure makes it easy to detach an 'atom' of light and to relocate it, separate from its colleagues. Each self-sufficient sphere is capable of shedding its own light for around four hours after being charged up. When the intensity begins to fade, simply plug the light module back into the base molecule for recharging. It's a fine, rare example of the scientific world inspiring the visual properties of design.

THIS BIOLOGICAL LAMP, BY THE BELGIAN DESIGNER MAARTEN DE CEULAER, HAS MORE THAN ONE TRICK UP ITS SLEEVE. IT CAN CHANGE SHAPE, BE TWISTED AND TURNED, AND BE ARRANGED INTO ANY POSITION. INFINITELY RENEWABLE, LIKE CELLS REPRODUCING, YOU'RE UNLIKELY TO TIRE OF THE NOMAD LIGHT MOLECULE.

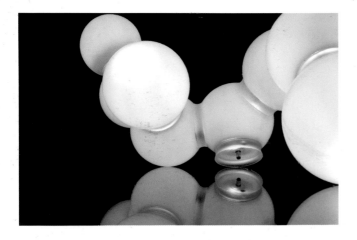

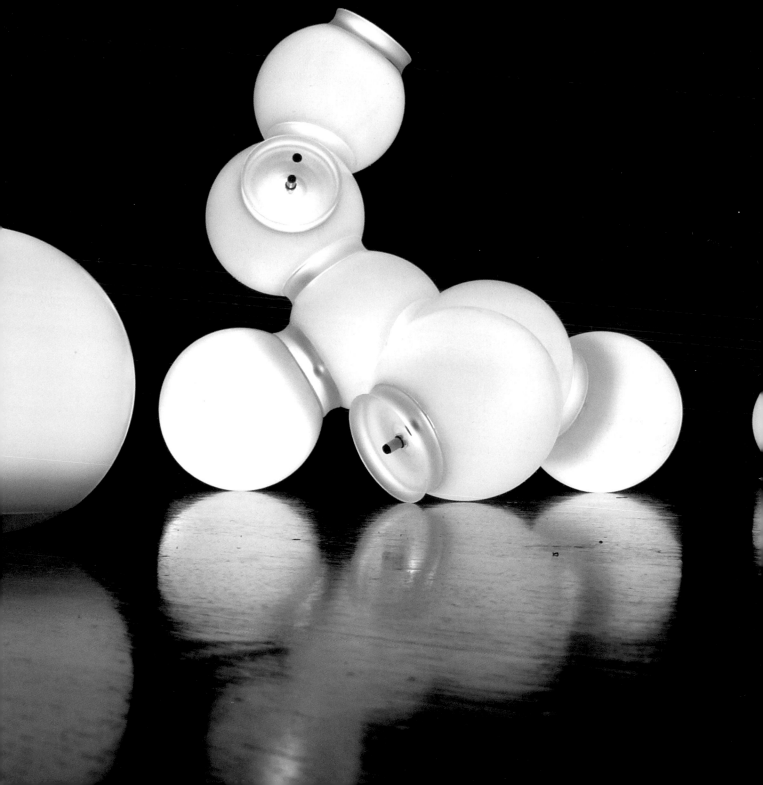

SLICED ARMCHAIR

Another blend of old and new, of tradition and innovation, the Empress chair was designed on a computer yet crafted entirely by hand. Each wooden strut was cut out and individually glued, creating an elegant yet challenging object. The Empress emerged from Julian Mayor's San Franciscan studio in 2003 with a statement from the designer explaining that the seat is "based on the shape of the human figure." We just hope it's more comfortable than it looks.

ANOTHER JULIAN MAYOR CREATION, THE IMPRESSION CHAIR, ORIGINALLY DATING FROM 2002, ENJOYED A REBIRTH AT THE MILAN EXHIBITION IN 2007, WHEN THE ARTIST AND DESIGNER PRESENTED A VERSION MADE OF ALUMINIUM.

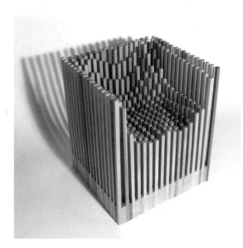

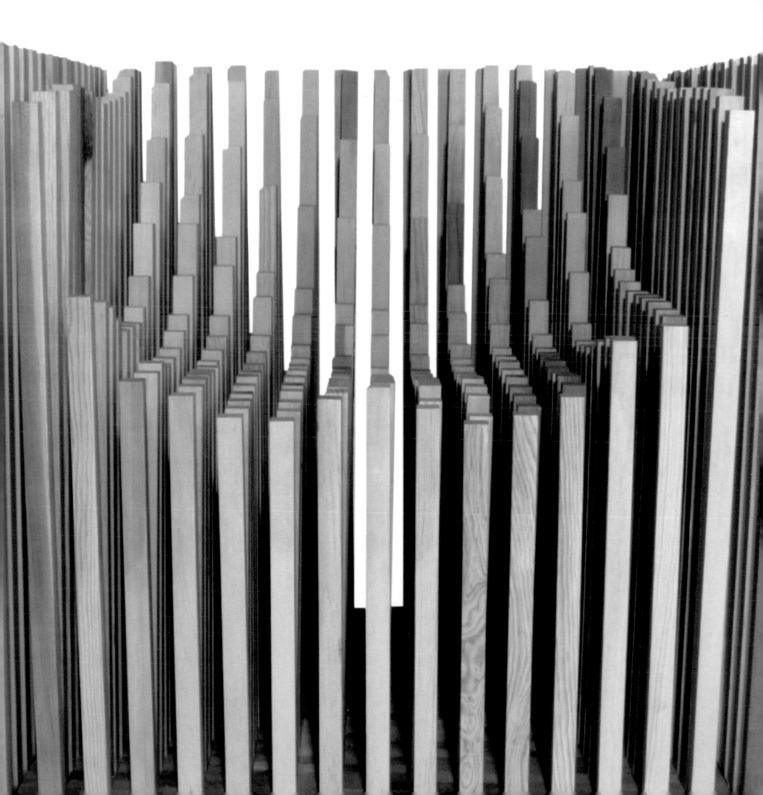

TRANSFORM

There's something particularly inspiring about taking neglected, everyday objects and radically adapting them to a new role; creating something spectacular, beautiful or just downright weird. That's how designers think – they study and contemplate the original function of an apparently trivial object, and then set their imagination to work on transforming the mundane into something sublime and unique. Surrealism, absurdity, even insanity – all can play a part in the creative processes that accompany transformation. In an age when, increasingly, lives and objects are formatted, globalised and standardised, the sense of the absurd that first inspired André Breton's surrealist movement in 1920s is finding new life in the design world.

DO HIT CHAIR

MARIJN VAN DER POLL

www.marijnvanderpoll.com

DO IT YOURSELF

Tough day at work? One day soon you might be able to unwind by smashing the life out of the Do Hit Chair. Created by Marijn van der Poll, the sacrificial seat is the perfect remedy for stress. The piece is made from 1.25mm thick steel plates, just waiting to be pummelled into shape (however random that shape might be). Marijn took his inspiration for the design from Enzo Mari's Sof-sof chair, creating what might be called a free interpretation. At present Marijn faces the perennial designer's dilemma: whether to keep the Do Hit Chair as a 'one-off' or to mass-produce it so that we might all feel the benefit.

THIS PIECE, CREATED IN 1999, WAS BOUGHT BY DROOG (WWW.DROOG.COM).

DRIP-LIGHT

A fine example of how design can transform the ordinary, the Lichtinfusion takes its inspiration from the intravenous drip stands found at hospital bedsides the world over. Architect and designer Christian Maas has brought a touch of humour to the object, breaking the rules of function and expertly catching our attention in the process. Hung from a steel base, the lamp is made up of four "bottles" of light, each linked to the supply cables by transparent wires.

BACKREST COAT HANGER

SUBVERTING THE ICONS

John Nouanesing takes subversion to the extreme. By placing objects out of context and beyond accepted, trusted rationale, he grabs our attention but also, once we've established what it is we're seeing ('A chair, cut-up and glued to the wall?'), gets us thinking about alternative functions for the objects we use everyday. Nouanesing also makes us ponder the permanence of objects and the afterlife they might enjoy once, in this instance, they cease to be chairs. The young French designer adds a certain frisson to the work by choosing to subvert established design classics, such as the Alessi chair, refigured here to form a collection of coat hangers.

EXPLOSIVE CHAMPAGNE

Specially created by Eric Berthes for the release of Quantum of Solace, and produced in a run of just 207, this top of the range collectors' presentation case is shaped like a bullet from the Walther PPK, signature gun of the most famous secret agent of them all, James Bond. Made in solid pewter, the case stands on a carbon-coated base... and conceals in its body a magnum of Bollinger La Grande Année 1999 champagne. Once the champagne has been quaffed, the giant bullet can be used as a canister (complete with leather-covered key) in which to keep jewellery, papers and the other accoutrements of a secret agent's life.

WHEN THE FIRST JAMES BOND MOVIES WERE MADE, A PARTNERSHIP AGREEMENT WAS SIGNED WITH THE CHAMPAGNE BRAND BOLLINGER, OR MORE PRECISELY BETWEEN CHRISTIAN BIZOT, THE DIRECTOR OF BOLLINGER, AND ALBERT R "CUBBY" BROCCOLI, PRODUCER OF THE FILMS.

PACKAGE HOLIDAY

Do you sometimes wish you could just pack the kids up in a box and post them to the other side of the world? Perhaps your better half would fit in the parcel too? This Human Packaging could help... or at least it could in theory (clearly, any actual attempt to package and ship your immediate family will draw the attention of social services, customs, the police, etc.). The work, l'être objet (the being-object), was conceived by Belgian designer Elric Petit, a member of the Big Game collective, for an exhibition on the theme of the survival object, and duly won a Vitra Belgium Award. Through the piece, Petit hopes to represent the transition from human to object.

MEASURING 140CM X 140CM X 80CM, THE SPECIAL BOX FOR HUMANS SEEMS INTENDED MORE FOR LITTLE PEOPLE.

CANDLELIT DINNER

Design collective L'Air de Rien have taken the humble coat hanger and transformed it into something that brilliantly transcends its original function. It still hangs, but now it illuminates as well. The mobile candleholders can be hung in solitude or built up, one on top of another, to create a gently spinning beacon over the dinner table. Perfect for those candlelit dinner parties on a winter's evening. It's even easy to store, slipping comfortably in the drawer when not in use. Just mind your head when you stand up to make a toast... and ease back a bit on the flammable hair spray.

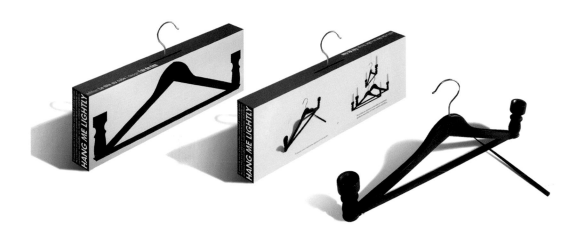

SAILING BATH

Established wisdom suggests that water should generally be kept outside the boat, which is why Wieki Somers' Bathboat makes such an immediate visual impression – few everyday objects have been so obviously and successfully subverted. The Dutch designer made the boats (in a run of thirty) using wood from her local forests, and fitted each with a plaque to be engraved with the name of the future owner. Wieki has made her name with work that transforms, but which also adds a poetic element to the objects involved. And, whilst the Bathboat is clearly functional, who would deny the poetry of the design. The 195cm-long tub is marketed by the Kreo Gallery.

WIEKI SOMERS WAS A PUPIL OF HELLA JONGERIUS AND GIJS BAKKER, THE FOUNDER OF DROOG. SHE BELONGS TO THE SECOND GENERATION OF DUTCH DESIGNERS. HER WORK OFTEN FOCUSES ON MATERIALS LIKE CERAMICS, AS SEEN IN THE BLOSSOMS VASE AND IN HER HIGH TEA TEAPOT, SHAPED LIKE A BOAR'S HEAD AND DECKED OUT IN A SMALL NUTRIA FUR COAT.

MAY I TAKE YOUR COAT?

The young German designer David Olschewski is a master of offbeat design. Here he takes the common-or-garden contents of the average shed and gives them a new, design-conscious function. Shovels and garden forks, mounted on elongated poles, serve amusingly as coat stands. David's catalogue reveals a similarly inventive collection of other work, from a stool made of swimming armbands, another stool made from broom-heads and a whole set of sitting room furniture based on a single object – a bathtub. All a brilliant amalgam of recycling and transformation.

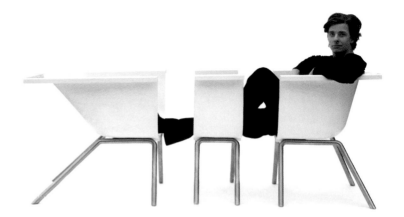

KEYBOARD BAG

Portuguese designer João Sabino's reinvention of the computer keyboard speaks for itself. The instantly familiar components look stunning out of context; radically shifting function and acquiring no small degree of aesthetic impact as they re-gather, disarranged, to adorn the conventionally shaped shopping bag. Each bag is made from 393 keys, backed with a black nylon inner. João, a graduate of the Escola Superior de Arte e Design, near Porto, has produced a number of other lauded products, including Bottled Spices, which reuse old glass bottles as storage devices, and the Helium Lamp, a large, illuminated sphere that hovers on the ceiling.

Available in pink, white, red or black.

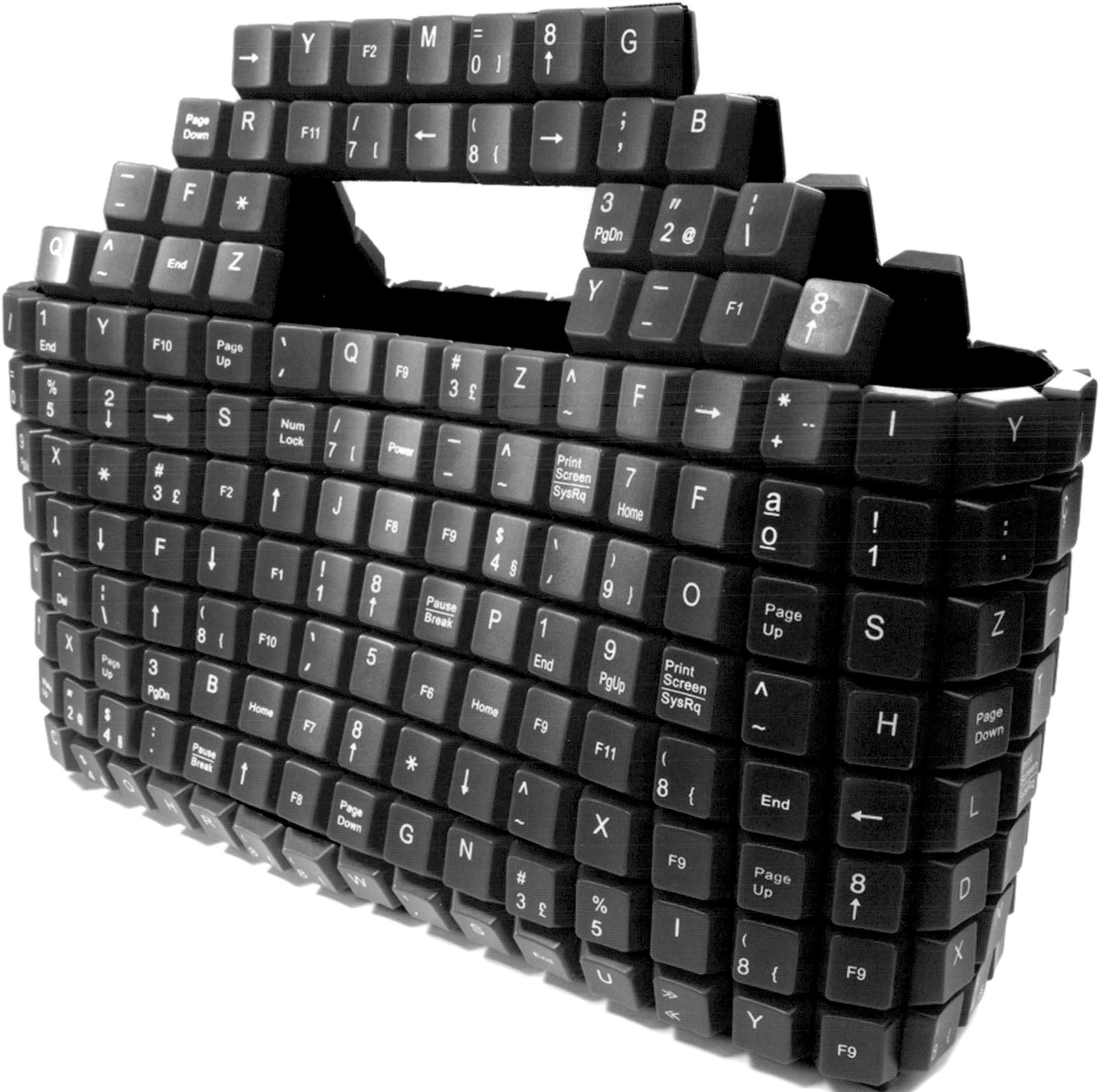

IDEAS FROM ATYPYK

Don't sell the fur

The old 'Welcome' mat gets a much-needed revamp with this, the bearskin doormat. Spread-eagled on the hallway floor, the bear's days of wandering around stealing picnics are clearly some way past, so why not make him feel useful - wipe your feet on him. The Bearskin mat (and it isn't 'real', in case you hadn't twigged), measuring 200cm x 225 cm, is typical of the offbeat Atypyk approach to design.

Bearskin
www.atypyk-e-shop.com

The cow fridge, a pistol ruler, the Déjeuner sur l'Herbe tablecloth, a break-up letter written indelibly on a handkerchief – each new object from the French collective Atypyk appears weirder than the last. The Atypyk agenda distorts or even ignores the rules, giving us small, sly nudges – a designer's name here, a vague description there – that offer little in the way of a meaningful insight into what is a striking body of work.

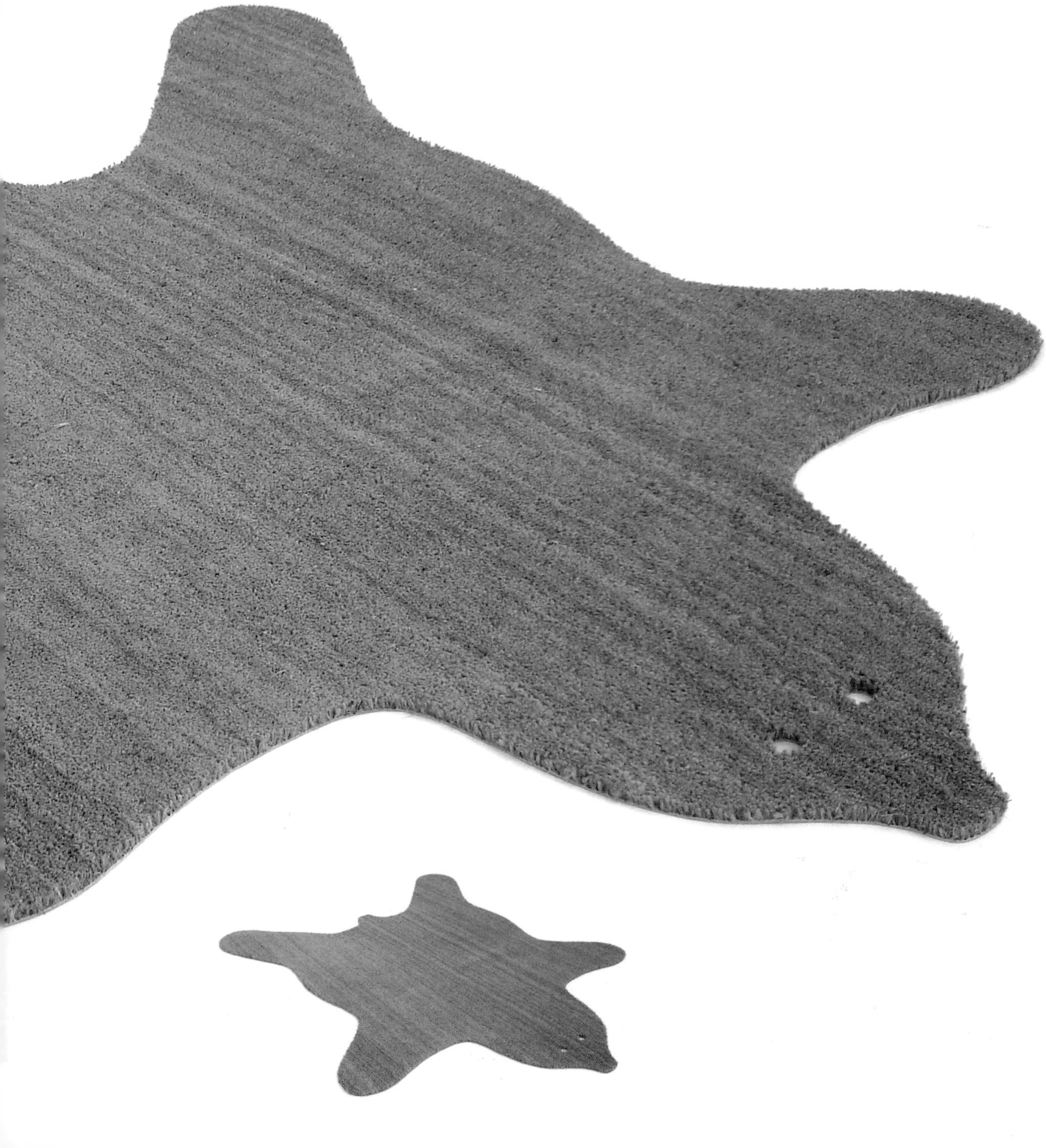

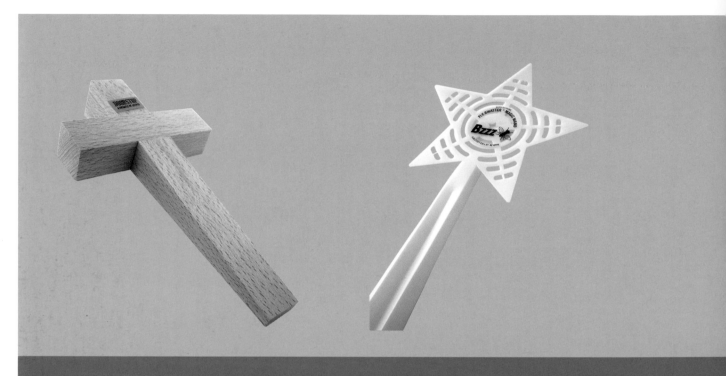

Alléluia !

The Atypyk Doorstop would bring a sense of piety to the most irreverent of thresholds. Made of solid beech, it hangs on the door handle when not in use. Every vestry should have one.

Doorstop
www.atypyk-e-shop.com

Magic fly-swatter

Hovering somewhere between subversion and stylish design, the Bzzz fly swatter brings a new (and not entirely appropriate) sense of fun to the killing of flies. It's girly, it's original, it's bad news for flies – what's not to like?

Bzzz
www.atypyk-e-shop.com

Knock-down

The Clumsy Coaster exemplifies the Atypyk sense of fun and originality. It might just disguise those marks you've got a nasty habit of leaving on other people's furniture and tablecloths.

Clumsy Coaster
www.atypyk-e-shop.com

Give your flowers a drink

Show the woman in your life how much you care: give her a vase made of beer cans. Alright, not a great idea, but you can't deny the 6Pack has a certain sense of humour. The plastic base is sold on the Atypyk website; the other bits – the flowers and beer cans – you have to find separately.

6Pack
www.atypyk-e-shop.com

NOT WAVING BUT DROWNING

The bathroom plug becomes a whirling maelstrom of danger with the Help! Drain Stopper. Only a despairing hand remains visible; the wretched final cry for help from whomever it is drowning in your pipe work. It takes something special to lift the drudgery of doing the dishes, but we're pretty sure this will do it. A word of caution though: don't be a hero - whoever's down there is beyond saving.

FRED & FRIENDS OFFER A RANGE OF OFFBEAT OBJECTS AND AMUSING ACCESSORIES FOR THE HOME. UNUSUAL CUTLERY, EAR KEY RINGS, TOOTH-SHAPED TOOTHBRUSH HOLDERS, THE MOUSETRAP CHEESEBOARD, A MANIC PAC-MAN, ICE CUBES SHAPED LIKE THE TITANIC FOR YOUR "GIN & TITONIC"... THE LIST IS LONG AND FUNNY – LEARN MORE ON THEIR WEBSITE.

HANDS UP!

You know you've hit rock bottom when inanimate objects start insulting you. But don't take offence from the marvellously fun Handjob Hooks when they give you the finger; enjoy, instead, the irreverent humour. Besides, most of the gestures are actually quite friendly – the thumbs up, handshake and OK sign, for example. Made from composite materials and finished in gloss paint, the realistic hands look bizarre but brilliant, emerging disembodied from the wall. They come in several colours, including black, pink, orange, red and white, all available direct from the designers.

EXPERTS IN THE ART OF SUBVERSION, YVES THELERMONT AND DAVID HUPTON SELL VARIOUS OTHER,
HIGHLY ORIGINAL CREATIONS ON THEIR WEBSITE: HAT STANDS IN THE SHAPE OF KITCHEN UTENSILS
COMING OUT OF THE WALL, BENT MUGS THAT SIT PERFECTLY ON YOUR KNEE AND, MORE RECENTLY,
HALOGEN LAMPS IN THE SHAPE OF ANIMALS.

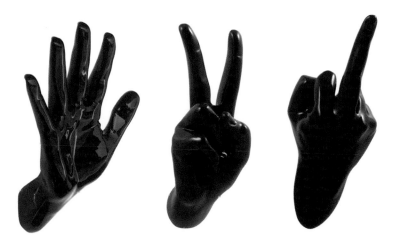

COLOUR CHANGE

Karim Rashid's modernistic Snap Chairs can't fail to brighten the home. Made of expanded polypropylene, the chairs have adjustable and inter-changeable seats, enabling one colour to be replaced with another. There are six colours in all, and with changes easily made you can play with the different combinations until you find something that works. Colourful, fu-turistic, organic, amusing and eccentric, the chairs are a fine reflection of their famous creator.

A MAJOR FIGURE IN CONTEMPORARY DESIGN, KARIM RASHID HAS WORKED WITH THE KEY INDUSTRY PLAYERS OF RECENT YEARS, FROM ISSEY MIYAKE TO TOMMY HILFIGER, SONY TO KENZO. HIS WORK INHABITS A COLOURFUL WORLD OF SENSUAL FORMS AND FUTURISTIC DÉCOR – WITNESS HIS INTERIORS AND DESIGNS FOR EVERYDAY OBJECTS, SUCH AS THE SLICE KNIFE.

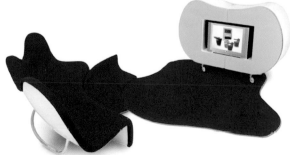

INFLATED IDEAS

Inflatables have come along way since the first Lilo slipped into the swimming pool. These days they've moved indoors and they're reliable. As these designs, created by Inflate in collaboration with Ron Arad, show, they're also deeply cool. Take the Inflate Lounge Chair for example: it looks like an abstract scorpion, raising its tail for a fight. Inflate also produce a range of inflatable cushions that combine these looks with practicality – they're easy to store and inflate (all you need is a vacuum cleaner) and endearingly comfortable to sit on.

NICK CROSBIE IS THE FOUNDER OF INFLATE, A COLLECTIVE THAT MADE ITS NAME WITH INFLATABLE DOMES, AND WHICH CONTINUES TO PUSH BOUNDARIES WITH INFLATABLE MATERIALS, OBJECTS AND STRUCTURES.

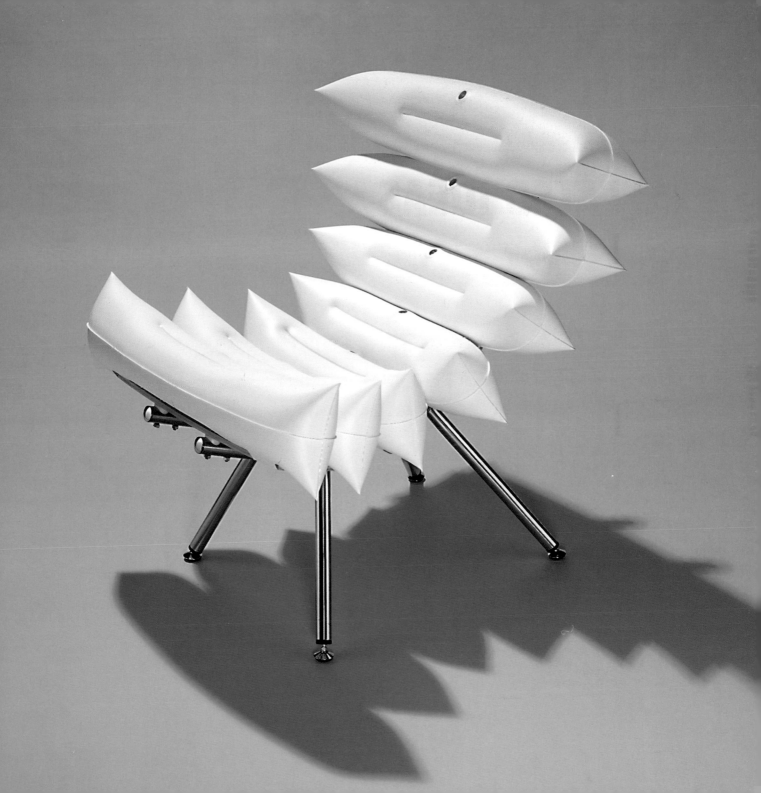

BELLE & BON

KONSTANTIN GRCIC www.konstantin-grcic.com

CRACKING GOOD EGG CUP

The boiled egg has spawned numerous inventive accessories over the years, most with a common aim – keeping the thing still whilst you devour it. The Belle & Bon egg cup from German designer Konstantin Grcic is surely amongst the most visually pleasing devices for keeping the humble egg in its place. Delicate, unfussy and practical, the Belle & Bon brings a poised elegance to this, the most functional of devices. The egg cups, made from hand-painted porcelain, and with varying colours at the end of the long stem, are sold with an equally elegant spoon.

KONSTANTIN GRCIC BEGAN HIS CAREER WITH JASPER MORRISON, BEFORE GOING SOLO. WIDELY RECOGNISED AND PRAISED, HIS DESIGNS HAVE BEEN EXHIBITED AT THE MOMA IN NEW YORK AND THE MUSÉE DES ARTS DÉCORATIFS IN PARIS. IN 2007, HE WAS CHOSEN AS DESIGNER OF THE YEAR BY *NOW! DESIGN À VIVRE* AT THE MAISON & OBJET EXHIBITION.

READING CHAIR

The Bibliochase takes curling up in a chair with a good book to a new level. Designed by Italians and sold by Nobody&co, the piece of furniture is both chair and library. The leather seat and back of the chair are built into the surrounding frame of bookshelves. You need never get up and reach for the shelves again; once you've finished a book, simply pick another one from the chair. As you might expect of such a bookish object, the Bibliochase is inherently intelligent, combining looks and function in one design. Apparently it holds five metres worth of books.

HATS OFF

Elevated from its traditional context (the top of the head), the bowler hat makes an immediate visual impact as a lampshade. As does its taller sibling, the top hat. Named the Jeeves and Wooster, the hats are lined with gold (bowler hat) and silver (top hat) thermoplastic paint and pierced with an electric cable, ready to take a fluorescent bulb. English designer Jake Phipps raises some interesting cultural questions by placing the bygone, iconic symbols of the British class divide – and a certain brand of eccentricity – in an entirely new light (literally).

INDEX OF OBJECTS

INDEX OF DESIGNERS

PHOTO CREDITS